The **Schemer** and the **Dreamer**

# LUIS PALAU

## THE Schemer AND THE DREAMER

### GOD'S WAY TO THE TOP

## Discovery House Publishers

*Books, music, and videos that feed the soul with the Word of God*

Box 3566 Grand Rapids, MI 49501

Discovery House is affiliated with RBC Ministries, Grand Rapids, Michigan 49512.

Discovery House books are distributed to the trade exclusively by Barbour Publishing, Inc., Uhrichsville, Ohio 44683.

**Library of Congress Cataloging-in-Publication Data**

---

Palau, Luis, 1934–
   The schemer and the dreamer : God's way to the top / by Luis Palau.
      p.   cm.
   Originally published: Portland, Or. : Multnomah Press, © 1976.
   ISBN 1-57293-048-9
   1. Jacob (Biblical patriarch) 2. Joseph (Son of Jacob)
3. Patriarchs (Bible)—Biography. 4. Bible. O.T.—Biography.
5. Christian life. I. Title.
BS573.P28   1999
222′.110922—dc21                                          98–48899
                                                            CIP

---

*Printed in the United States of America*

99  01  03  02  00
CHG
1  3  5  7  9  10  8  6  4  2

# Contents

# Chapter 1

# *The Grabber*

*He did it with Jacob!* It took Him about 100 years, but He did it. He's done it with everyone who belongs to Jesus Christ. God has begun a work in your life—and He's going to finish it. Does that excite you as it does me?

When God begins to work in a person's life, He never quits. He's determined. He *will* finish the job. There's no getting away from the fact. Doesn't Philippians 1:6 say, "being confident of this, that he who began a good work in you will carry it on to completion until the day of Christ Jesus"?

The desire of God is to make me as a man and you as a man or woman just like Jesus Christ—to build the character of Christ in us. God has purposed to do that. Galatians 4:19 says, "My dear children, for whom I am again in the pains of childbirth until Christ is formed in you . . . ." What God did with Jacob, He's trying to do with us—all of us. God was continually trying to mold Jacob into the man He wanted him to be, trying to build *His* character into the man and make him a complete person. What a job God took upon Himself! This man Jacob had to be one of the most stubborn men who ever lived.

Because the Old Testament was written for our example and warning (1 Corinthians 10:11), we see ourselves in it so often. We begin to suspect what God might be trying to do in *our* lives and the lives of our families, when we see what He did in the lives of those Old Testament characters.

No matter how much your wife has been trying to work you over and you've been resisting because you're stubborn and self-assured—no matter how strongly God has been trying to speak to you through an individual or through His Word and you've refused to listen—*God is going to have His way in your life.* "The one who calls you is faithful and he will do it" (1 Thessalonians 5:24), no matter how stubborn we are. What a challenge to the Lord as He works with some of us!

God is God. God is King. God is at work with nations and with individuals. The fascinating thing is that He always reveals, at least in general outline form, what He intends to do. Watch for this as we trace Jacob's beginnings.

Isaac was forty years old when he married Rebekah, the daughter of Bethuel and Aramean from Paddam-aram, sister of Laban. Isaac pleaded with Jehovah to give Rebekah a child, for even after many years of marriage she had no children. Then at last she became pregnant. And it seemed as though children were fighting each other inside her!

"I can't endure this," she exclaimed. So she asked the Lord about it.

And he told her, "The sons in your womb shall become two rival nations. One will be stronger than the other; and the older shall be a servant of the younger!"

And sure enough, she had twins. The first was born so covered with reddish hair that one would think he was wearing a fur coat! So they called him "Esau" [meaning "hairy"]. Then the other twin was born with his hand on Esau's heel! So they called him Jacob (meaning "Grabber"). Isaac was sixty years old when the twins were born (Genesis 25:20–26 TLB).

Jacob, you're going to discover, is a lot like you and me. He is especially like people who are climbing the ladder of success. Above him he sees other climbers, and his name isn't "Jacob" for nothing. That name actually means, "He shall grab by the heel." Watch out above! Watch out below!

But the life of Jacob isn't in the Bible to give us a lot of amusement so we can say, "Hey, Jacob. Way to go!" And it's not there just to show us that a fellow reaps what he sows. Beyond Jacob we see God's character as He reveals Himself in the life of the man.

You want to know what God is really like? You can find out by reading a volume on the theology of God and His attributes or you can read through the Bible and see Him work in the lives of people—people like Jacob and Joseph. This is the primary way God chooses to reveal Himself.

Are you willing to see God just as He shows Himself? That's the crucial question. Are you ready to discover what He thinks of Himself? He says, "I am God, and not man . . ." (Hosea 11:9). If you really desire to know God as He is, let Him speak for Himself as He does in the lives of Jacob and Joseph. Whether you listen and make Him Lord of your life is then your choice.

But you say, "Hey, it's okay to look at God's character, but right now I've got a business that's going bankrupt and my wife is giving me trouble." Or you say, "My husband is about to leave me—so what's all this talk about God's character? Why don't you talk about the family and its problems instead?"

I believe that as we review Jacob and his family and the way he provoked such turmoil within it, we'll learn quite a bit about the family—yours and mine.

God can work with people at all levels. He can work with many nations, and He can work with one nation. He can work with the president of a nation and he can deal with all the people individually or as a mass all at the same time, because God is God.

In the Old Testament, we see God revealing Himself and His purposes, and we realize that a sovereign God has the reins of the governments of the world in His hands. That's exciting!

The Lord tells Rebekah, "Two nations are in your womb, and two peoples from within you will be separated; one people will be stronger than the other, and the older will serve the younger" (Genesis 25:23).

Two sons, unborn, and God is declaring what will happen in their lives. This is God's foreknowledge in action. He knows the end from the beginning. He saw those two little sons of Rebekah and Isaac when they were conceived and He determined what they were going to be. Against all tradition and nature, the younger would dominate over the older.

God knows each one of us before we're born. Jeremiah 1:5 says, "Before I formed you in the womb I knew you, before you were born I set you apart; I appointed you as a prophet to the nations." To think that before I was born in Argentina back in 1934, God knew me, Luis Palau. Me! Out of millions of people! Fantastic thought! He planned that I would preach the gospel. Before I knew my own name, God knew me!

Further, God says, "Before you were born, I separated you." While we were yet inside our mothers, God set a plan for our lives.

That's exactly what God was doing there in Genesis. He had plans for Jacob and Esau. He saw their lives unfold before they were even born. He worked out His purposes year after year in their lives, just as He does in yours.

### God delights to let us in on the plans

We see God interested in fulfilling *His* purposes through Jacob—in His own *divine* way. Jacob was also interested in fulfilling God's purpose through him. Can you guess how? His *own* way, of course. Jacob's natural way. That was Jacob's problem for 100 years.

When Jacob's life was almost over, his son Joseph took him to the Pharaoh of Egypt. Then Pharaoh asked Jacob, "How old are you?" and our man Jacob sadly had to answer, "The years of my pilgrimage are a hundred and thirty . . . . My years have been few and difficult" (Genesis 47:9).

What a way to end a life! A man reaches 130 and, when he's asked his age, he has to say, "Few and difficult are the days and years . . . ." They seemed like few because he had wrecked and wasted them so badly. He had so little to rejoice over, so few victorious memories; and they certainly were "difficult."

God knew about those two little boys inside their mother Rebekah. He gave warning that they would be enemies. God is a self-revealing God. He loves to reveal Himself and His purposes; He doesn't hide Himself from man. If someone says, "I've been looking for God and I can't find Him," that person has just been looking in the wrong place. Since God's desire is to know you and be known by you, He has revealed Himself.

So when Rebekah, desperate at the fighting boys inside her, asked, "Lord, what's going on?" God spoke to her in a prophecy. He told her what was in store.

God would be glad to reveal His purposes to the whole world, if the world cared to listen; but He also takes pleasure in speaking to us in a personal way. Every Christian has the privilege to be able to talk with God, to spend time with Him and hear His voice—not necessarily in an audible way (although He can do that if He chooses) but through the Bible and through the indwelling Holy Spirit. God loves to build His people.

Psalm 32:8 says, "I will instruct you and teach you in the way you should go; I will counsel you and watch over you."

In that passage, God says, in effect, "Listen, I want to be your counselor. I want to guide you. I want to have my own eye upon you, your family, and your life. Don't be like a horse or a mule which one must direct with a whip and a bridle. If you'll be sensitive to me, I will direct you in a tender, quiet way all through your life."

If you feel as if God never speaks to you, take a little time off and allow Him to speak to your heart through the Bible. God does have a purpose for your life and for every person on this planet—man, woman, teenager . . . especially teenagers.

In the Bible, in almost every case, God began to work noticeably with men and women when they were young—sometimes when they were only six or seven years old, like Samuel (1 Samuel 2:19–4:1). God seems to love picking a person up when he is very young and guiding him all through life. Are you a candidate for just such a life?

## What about man's free will?

Parallel with the sovereignty of God, who ultimately fulfills all His purposes, man has a singular measure of responsibility. In Genesis 25:27–34, we find Esau fully exercising his will. Hear how the New Living Translation Bible puts it:

> As the boys grew up, Esau became a skillful hunter, a man of the open fields, while Jacob was the kind of person who liked to stay at home. Isaac loved Esau in particular because of the wild game he brought home, but Rebekah favored Jacob.
>
> One day when Jacob was cooking some stew, Esau arrived home exhausted and hungry from a hunt. Esau said to Jacob, "I'm starved! Give me some of that red stew you've made." (This was how Esau got his other name, Edom—"Red.")
>
> Jacob replied, "All right, but trade me your birthright for it."
>
> "Look, I'm dying of starvation!" said Esau. "What good is my birthright to me now?"
>
> So Jacob insisted, "Well then, swear to me right now that it is mine." So Esau swore an oath, thereby selling all his rights as the firstborn to his younger brother. Then Jacob gave Esau some bread and lentil stew. Esau ate and drank and went on about his business, indifferent to the fact that he had given up his birthright.

What God had foretold before these two were born, Esau himself freely confirmed by despising his birthright. He sealed the prediction of his own free will. God had announced that this would happen but didn't give details. In a moment of passion, Esau ruined his hour of opportunity just to fill his belly. What a momentous decision! Watch those moments of desperate impulse in your life.

Discussion about the sovereignty of God and the free will of man always raises this question: Where does the sovereignty of God end and the free will of man begin?

The answer? The sovereignty of God never ends. He is always sovereign. The will of man begins where God declares it should begin, and it ends when He wants it to end. God is God! He sets the limits where He pleases. Of course, He does it with perfect knowledge and wisdom; so don't panic. God is always good, and he is always God (Psalm 34:8–9).

Suppose some ants build a small anthill in my backyard. The ants climb all over the place. They eat on bushes my wife has tended so carefully. They build their home and hide food for the winter. As far as they're concerned, they run the world because they're free.

However, they are free in my backyard only as long as I let them be free. As long as I give them freedom to eat up my wife's bushes, store up food and do what they want, they're free.

However, the moment I say, "Okay, it's all over," and choose to get rid of them, that's the end of the ants. I am sovereign over my backyard. I bought it. They didn't. I'll give them freedom as long as I want.

That is a tiny picture of God at work in our lives. He never ceases to be sovereign. He tells us, "Listen, within these bounds, you are free to choose. Now choose." Our responsibility begins where He declares it begins. It ends when He says, "That's it."

God allowed Jacob to actually cheat his brother on a business deal. He wasn't in favor of it. He simply permitted it. He'll deal with Jacob and his cheating later.

Take another situation. God profoundly hates divorce. He could not have declared it more strongly in the Bible, yet He allows it. It's within His permissive will. He still hates it with a holy hatred, but He allows it because of the sinfulness of the race. So here, too, with Jacob's cheating. The consequences of breaking God's revealed will always hound us. You never fully get away from them. Galatians 6:7–8 declares, "Do not be deceived: God cannot be mocked. A man reaps what he sows. The one who sows to please his sinful nature, from that nature will reap destruction; the one who sows to please the Spirit, from the Spirit will reap eternal life."

### Isaac and Rebekah—what examples!

Esau's parents gave a very poor example to their sons. They were really something else, Isaac and Rebekah. Perhaps it was the way Rebekah was chosen to be Isaac's wife that got their marriage off to a bad start. Some people think it was a great example. Maybe it wasn't such a good idea to send a servant to find Isaac a wife, somewhere in the middle of nowhere. They were thrown together sight unseen. Not even Abraham knew the girl before the marriage. The home that produced Laban must have affected Rebekah, for both of them lied and cheated in later life.

Obviously, there was tremendous division in this home. You can safely say that this marriage wasn't at all what it should have been. Esau was loved by his father Isaac mostly because he cooked the nice little stews Isaac liked (Genesis 25:28). Which shows how mature Isaac was! Their mother, Rebekah, liked Jacob better—probably because her husband liked Esau. No specific reasons are given, but obviously they didn't see eye to eye.

We should help each other eliminate favoritism. It is a frightening streak in any family. Here it was demolishing.

Isaac was a weakling. A sensuous, indulgent lover of his stomach. He loved his son for his athletic skills and his cooking ability—weak reasons to love a son. And his most loved one, Esau, who considered his hunger more important than his birthright, followed Isaac's example—much to his own hurt. The result was that, humanly speaking, Isaac and Rebekah provoked many problems with their two boys by their own emotional favoritism.

### Don't lay all the blame on the parents

Yet the bulk of the responsibility for his actions falls on Esau, not on Isaac. Even if you have a weak father, a finger-licking, food-loving father, a father with a drinking problem, a mother with a temper, God will not permit you to blame them for your mistakes. The Bible places the whole responsibility on Esau. The individual is responsible before God and man.

Many people seeking counsel today unbiblically put too much responsibility for their own evil deeds on the parents, instead of where it belongs, on the doer of the evil deed. "The son will not share the guilt of the father, nor will the father share the guilt of the son" (Ezekiel 18:20).

I have made many mistakes. I wouldn't dare blame my mother or my father for them. My mistakes are not their fault. Anyone who wants to blame his parents for his weaknesses or his sins is a sad case. He's never going to find answers.

There's a book by Jay Adams on personal problems that I recommend reading. It is titled *The Christian Counselor's Manual* (Zondervan, 1986). In it he really blasts those who try to blame a weak mother or a strong father for their homosexuality. People use hundreds of excuses for homosexuality, as for so many other sins. Some say they are homosexuals because "the father was too strong"—some "because he was too weak." The mother was "too domineering"—she was "too weak." They always have an excuse. But the Bible places the responsibility directly on the individual, not on his parents. The biblical emphasis is always on individual responsibility. First, "All have sinned" (Romans 3:23). Second, "The wages of sin is death" (Romans 6:23). And, finally, "The soul who sins is the one who will die" (Ezekiel 18:4), not that person's parents!

Esau had his dreams, but threw them away in one burst of passion. He was hungry, he smelled good food, he despised everything that God would have given him. And as for Jacob, God would have found a way to fulfill His divine purposes for Jacob otherwise. But in a moment of desperate hunger Esau despised what God offered him.

How many young persons—and not-so-young—have ruined what God had for them in one moment of passionate desperation? Maybe a food temptation, perhaps a sexual passion or a money-grabbing opportunity. How many people, brought up in good environments, have in one blast of self-indulgence wreaked havoc in their lives and homes? Esau did just that.

### That first sin marks you

Jacob too had already begun a long, bitter path downward. His first evil act marked him for life. If you could remember the first sin you committed as a child, it's probably the sin that has kept dragging you down all through your life. Deal with it radically now!

Jacob did not deal with it. He kept trying to promote God's purposes in his own commercial way. He began to demonstrate a characteristic so many of us show in our business and daily life: guile. He was a scheming man. He was cunning, deceitful, sneaky, sly . . . he was a "Grabber" . . . how appropriate his very name.

Jacob was interested in success. He wasn't intent on sinning, yet he failed so badly. Why? Jacob wasn't a gross sinner; he was a nice person. Apparently he never committed immorality. Why? He never thought of abandoning his wife. He loved her. But he was a gross failure. Why? Because he tried to promote God's plans in his own way, not God's way. That was his lifelong problem. How much better had Jacob prayed with Jeremiah: "I know, O LORD, that a man's life is not his own; it is not for man to direct his steps. Correct me, LORD . . ." (Jeremiah 10:23–24).

## Such a good deal!

With Jacob, the descent began when he saw his brother hungry and said to himself, "Business is business. I'm going to get him!" And he did.

Then, because he was a "mama's boy," he probably went home gloating, "Mama, I did it. I did it. I got him in a moment of weakness. It was all fair and square and I got him! Esau turned over the birthright to me. Nobody can accuse me of any shady dealing. It was out in the open. A clean deal."

But it wasn't. It wasn't God's way of giving him the authority he so badly wanted. Many of us had tremendous promise when we were young. Twenty years later, we're still nothing for God. Why? We've tried to promote what God obviously gave us to do with the tactics

of the natural man—our essential unsaved self that con-
nives to get its own way. Romans 8:8 declares: "Those
controlled by the sinful nature cannot please God."
Twisting arms and trying to finagle and talk people into
things is God's work done man's way. It is not worth it.
It takes you nowhere. Never try it. You'll waste your
years. And as Catherine Booth, co-founder of the
Salvation Army, once wrote a girl: "Young woman, you
have not the right to waste your life."

That's what poor Jacob tried to do. Joseph, his son,
must have been observing him as he grew up. Joseph
must have profited from his father's error, for never once
did he promote God's purposes with the tactics of the
flesh. And he became the greatest. No so with his father.

## Don't try to twist God's arm

God is very patient. When Jacob committed this
sneaky, sly business transaction, God didn't send a bolt
of lightning. He didn't send a car (or camel) down the
road to run him down. God has plenty of time. He was
around before you and I were born and He's going to be
around when we are gone from this earth. The only ones
who can't afford to lose time are you and I. God has all
the time in the world; and He states, "I have loved you
with an everlasting love; I have drawn you with loving-
kindness" (Jeremiah 31:3).

All of us, when we feel that God has shown us the
road that we're to follow, run the risk of trying to implement God's revealed plan with carnal methods. From
my youth, I feel that I have known by the internal witness of the Holy Spirit and the statements of trustworthy
members of the body of Christ, that God has called me
to evangelize in the great cities of the world—to the

masses—through radio and television, literature and citywide evangelistic crusades.

Much has been accomplished by His grace. Millions have heard the gospel, many thousands have come to Christ. The Lord has allowed us to proclaim His gospel in scores of countries on six continents. Recently, we've even been able to minister in the Middle East, which has long been a great desire of mine. Yet so many doors still need to be opened!

But when it seems as if God is going a little slower than I want Him to go (and that happens quite often, because I'm rather aggressive and impatient and goal-conscious), I risk the dangers of trying to twist God's arm to get things moving a little faster, of stepping on individuals and of hurting people. All of this to advance *His plan* in my life you understand—of course! It is so subtle a temptation. But God deliver me! His way is that peaceful way of Proverbs 3:5–7, "Trust in the LORD with all your heart, and lean not on your own understanding; in all your ways acknowledge him, and he will make your paths straight. Do not be wise in your own eyes; fear the LORD and shun evil."

If only Jacob could have learned that. As Lord Byron put it, "Ah, what a tangled web we weave, when first we practice to deceive." What a tangled web! For Jacob, it was "some red stuff." What are you getting entangled in?

There's no need to be all tangled up. With all your heart, trust in the Lord. Don't lean on your own understanding. Acknowledge Him in all your ways and He will direct your paths. You don't have to twist God's arm. He can take care of His purposes for us better than we can. "Taste and see that the LORD is good!" exclaimed

David. "Blessed is the man who takes refuge in him" (Psalm 34:8).

God can do in one day what would take a hundred years of trying to do on our own. How foolish we are when we think we can further God's purposes with our own wits and wisdom. We can't.

This is the time when the words of a poet, echoing Philippians 2:5–11, can become a functional reality:

> He is Lord, He is Lord,
> He is risen from the dead and He is Lord.
> Every knee shall bow,
> Every tongue confess
> That Jesus Christ is Lord.

Is Jesus Christ the Lord of my ambitions? If only Jacob had asked himself that question *before* he acted!

# Chapter 2

# *The Bargainer*

*One sin leads to another*—we all know that. First, Jacob's doubtful "business deal" over the birthright. Next, both mother and son move on to outright deception of the old patriarch, Isaac. Although the evidence would not have condemned Jacob for the "business deal" with Esau, the incident did in very short order precipitate Jacob—with his mother—to make a bad thing worse. And this second downward step is unquestionably condemnable. That is the frightful reality: *One unsettled sin leads to another.*

Rebekah just happens to be listening at the door of the tent and hears Isaac arranging to give his blessing to Esau. *This will never do,* she thinks to herself. Hurriedly she calls for Jacob. Genesis 27:5–13 (NLT) tells the story:

> Rebecca overheard the conversation. So when Esau left to hunt for the wild game, she said to her son Jacob, "I overheard your father asking Esau to prepare him a delicious meal of wild game. He wants to bless Esau in the LORD's presence before he dies. Now, my son, do exactly as I tell you. Go out to the flocks and bring me two fine young goats. I'll prepare your father's favorite

dish from them. Take the food to your father; then he can eat it and bless you instead of Esau before he dies."

"But Mother!" Jacob replied. "He won't be fooled that easily. Think how hairy Esau is and how smooth my skin is! What if my father touches me? He'll see that I'm trying to trick him, and then he'll curse me instead of blessing me."

"Let the curse fall on me, dear son," said Rebekah. "Just do what I tell you. Go out and get the goats."

They did it too. They pulled it off. They fooled Isaac with goat skins and goat stew, tricking him into giving the blessing meant for the oldest son Esau to Jacob, the younger.

### Somebody made me do it!

The fact that his mother commanded Jacob to steal Esau's blessing did not let Jacob off the hook. He could not turn to the Lord on the day of reckoning and say, "But Lord, it wasn't really me. It was Mama who told me to do it. What could I do?" He was ultimately, unalterably responsible.

There is a point at which you should not obey your parents. That point is where they ask you to lie, cheat, or do anything that is wrong. According to the Word of God, "We must obey God rather than men" (Acts 5:29) at that point.

However, Jacob apparently agreed with Rebekah. He thought to himself, *Mother is right. If we don't hurry and make this deal, Esau will come back with venison. He'll cook it just like our father likes it. Isaac will eat and drink and give Esau the blessing. Then all God's plans for me will fall apart. We must help God out.* In essence, by his actions, that is what he concluded in his own heart and mind.

Jacob might have thought, *If I don't get that blessing, God's plans will not be fulfilled. In fact, God may be dishonored. Then what would happen? We really have to do what we can. The end justifies the means in a case like this.*

Many of us have been confronted with the choice of how far we should obey others. I remember when I worked in a bank in my country in South America. This was an international bank and I advanced rapidly because I knew English as well as Spanish.

They placed me in the foreign department. We had to make many business transactions in foreign currency, which is the best place to make money deceitfully. And, sad to say, the management and employees played many tricks on the clients every day.

Say the city officials bought three million dollars worth of machinery in Chicago. They would have to pay in local pesos. The exchange rate might be 42. The bank would say to the man who came from the city, "Today the dollar is worth 45." This meant that for every dollar, the bank was making three pesos dishonestly, in addition to the regular one percent commission for the transaction. Multiply that by three million dollars. That's nine million pesos we made in a thirty-minute transaction.

When I first began to work, I would check with the manager, "What's the exchange rate today?"

He'd think a while and say, "Tell him it's 45."

I didn't ask questions, but I began to realize we were not being honest. The city officials couldn't do anything; they trusted the bank. The fact was, we were cheating people out of millions of pesos every month.

Finally, when he thought he had my confidence, the manager said to me, "Well, you know, the deal is this . . ." and explained the scheme.

Then one Sunday afternoon I was preaching the gospel on the street corner. "If you come to Christ, He'll fill your heart," I was saying. "If you come to Christ, He'll give you power. If you come to Christ, you'll overcome temptation. You'll be clean. You'll be able to live a wonderful life, out in the open . . . ."

Suddenly I heard this little voice inside me, saying, "Hey, Luis, this sounds great. You're really preaching the gospel. But do you remember last week when that man came to the bank and bought American dollars? You told him the rate was 47 when it was really 45. How can you reconcile that with your beautiful preaching to this little crowd at this street corner?"

I kept on preaching and gave the invitation. But when I went back to my room, it began to haunt me. Finally one day, I worked up courage and went to the manager. "Do we always have to cheat this way until we get to the top? Is this the way it's going to be?" I asked.

"What do you mean, *cheat?*" he bellowed. He got red in the face.

"This deal we pull with people isn't right," I said. "We're deceiving people." I tried to be as humble as I knew how; but nervous as I was, I began to feel good inside.

"Now, listen," he said. "I do it because I get orders from above. You do it because I tell you to. Don't ask any questions. It's not your responsibility. You're just doing what I tell you."

"I just can't do it." I told him. "I can't lie to people even if orders do come impersonally from the top."

He went into a real tirade then. "Look man, we've been training you. We've got big plans for you. Now you're telling me we're a bunch of liars? You're accusing me of being a cheat?"

"No, sir, I'm just telling you I can't do it."

"Well, if you can't do it, you've had it! This is the way it is. You're not on the Board of Directors. You are an employee. Who cares who made the decision?"

Well, as far as I was concerned, I had to resign from that bank. It seemed like a tragedy because I had a widowed mother, five sisters, and a little brother to support. But I resigned.

However, the Lord had an open door for me—the ministry of full-time gospel preaching. So what appeared to be a tragedy and a temptation to compromise for a little longer because of financial pressures, the Lord used to bring me out of the bank and into the work He had prepared for me. How I praise Him for doing it that way—His way!

### Fear haunts the deceiver

Jacob probably went through this type of temptation. But it never pays to do the wrong thing to accomplish the right ends. It *never* pays.

You notice that immediately after Jacob's deception, the horror and fear set in. Whenever you cheat or deceive or lie, a horror settles on your soul; and it never leaves again until you've settled the problem.

Kipling once said, "Nothing is ever settled until it is settled right." If a person is deceptive and cheats, whether it's on a husband or a wife or in business or whatever, he feels a horror and fear that haunts him for the rest of his life or until the day when he settles it with God and man.

The first person to panic was Rebekah. The moment she heard that Esau was planning to kill her boy, she hurriedly called Jacob. Those two then made a third shady move. One sin leads to another. They lied to Isaac. Then, using the excuse that Jacob would never find a decent wife if he stayed around there, Rebekah cleared the way for Jacob to leave to go wife-hunting. Actually, Jacob was running away.

Many people who experience what is commonly called a "breakdown," do so because they are trying to run away from some horrible covered-up thing, something they're trying to cover up instead of fix up.

Dr. William Glasser in his book, *Reality Therapy*, cites illustration after illustration of people who remain in the security of mental institutions simply because they refuse to face reality.

### Don't worry! God is God

Notice the illustration of how the government of God operates:

1. Isaac, the father, got what he deserved. He was a weakling who appeared to love his son mainly because of his cooking skills. He set himself up for it by his immature favoritism.

2. Esau "asked for it" and got it because he had rejected his rightful privileges some time before.

3. Jacob paid dearly for his deception—he wasted the best twenty years of his life as a result. It wasn't worth it, was it?

4. Finally, Rebekah, the mother, never saw her favorite son again. She died before the deceiver she favored returned with his ill-gotten gains.

That's the way the government of God operates.

Many times it seems that everything is out of control—in your family, the church or the world. But it really isn't. God is in control of the whole affair and of everyone within the situation. He so governs the universe that everyone gets what's coming to him, good or bad. For God is God. Don't worry. He knows how to take care of all situations.

At the time it seemed as if Jacob had gotten away with his scheme. But he hadn't. He never did enjoy any benefits from his shady dealings. It was a total waste of time—a shameful use of a young life.

### Paul, don't go

Why do we try to implement God's plan man's way? And why is it that all of us try? The apostle Paul did this and paid dearly, too. Sometimes we don't like to mention the negatives about old Paul's life, but he made some crucial mistakes. He was human, you know!

Now God used Paul's error because He always does. God is going to accomplish His purposes, no matter what—no matter what mistakes we make or sins we commit or how disobedient we persist on being. When God says He's going to do something, He does it! But we reap the harvest of our mistakes.

Paul paid for his mistake. God used it for good, yes, certainly. That is His way, always. "We know that in all things God works for the good of those who love him, who have been called according to his purpose" (Romans 8:28). But that does not mean it is God's best for us.

### Face to face—with God

We have seen the third step in Jacob's bitter, downhill road. He and his mother schemed and plotted, not trusting God's plan for their lives. Now God Almighty is bringing Jacob to the place where, for the very first time,

Jacob meets God—face to face. For despite it all, God loved this young man. He said, "Yet I have loved Jacob" (Malachi 1:3).

Genesis 28:10–15 (TLB) reads:

> Jacob left Beersheba and traveled toward Haran. At sundown he arrived at a good place to set up camp and stopped there for the night. Jacob found a stone for a pillow and lay down to sleep. As he slept, he dreamed of a stairway that reached from earth to heaven. And he saw the angels of God going up and down on it.
>
> At the top of the stairway stood the LORD, and he said, "I am the LORD, the God of your grandfather Abraham and the God of your father, Isaac. The ground you are lying on belongs to you. I will give it to you and your descendants. Your descendants will be as numerous as the dust of the earth! They will cover the land from east to west and from north to south. All the families of the earth will be blessed through you and your descendants. What's more, I will be with you, and I will protect you wherever you go. I will someday bring you safely back to this land. I will be with you constantly until I have finished giving you everything I have promised."

Isn't that a fantastic affirmation from God? This reveals the faithfulness of God's character (John 15:14–15, Ephesians 2:10, Hebrews 13:5–6). I believe that God wills to do the same with every one of us. If we are married, He speaks to us as a family. If we are single, as individuals. Jacob was, at this point, unmarried. God speaks to Jacob of his descendants—his family. If you trust Him as a single, then when you are ready to get married, He will bring into your life someone to whom He's already shown the same direction that He's shown you. He would have done so for Jacob, had he rested in Jehovah, rather than trusting in his own schemes.

## Scripture speaks

The Holy Spirit takes Scripture and speaks directly to the heart. He says to you specifically, "I want to do this and this and this with your life. I *will* do it. I have promised it. If you will only *let* me, there is no limit to what I'm ready to do through your life."

What has God said to you personally, by way of promise? Have you spent enough time in the presence of God? Alone or as a couple, are you letting God speak to you? Letting Him impress you through Scripture by the Holy Spirit, by some other circumstantial means or by another member of the body of Christ with something He wants to show you? "Wait for the LORD," says David, "be strong and take heart and wait for the LORD" (Psalm 27:14) . . . and make Psalm 62 your own.

God Almighty met Jacob, stood before him, Scripture shows, and gave him tremendous "personalized" promises. God gave similar promise to several others, both before and following Jacob; but this was Jacob's hour alone with God. Have you had such an hour of encounter?

## Never too late

Years ago the Lord spoke to me through a verse in Isaiah, chapter 48, verse 18:

> If only you had paid attention to my commands, your peace would have been like a river.

Isn't that what everyone really wants in his daily life? An inner peace? Peace like a river? Quiet and steady. There's something about a peaceful river!

"If only you had paid attention to my commands . . . ." The Lord is crying out in a sort of divine anguish.

"To think that I've given people this enormous book full of instructions and promises and tremendous truth. Oh, that you would hearken to it! Then your peace would be like a river . . . ."

Some time ago I was talking with a man who is now my friend. We sat alone for a while, just chatting. Then he began telling me some of his story and it literally broke me up. Somehow this man reminded me of one of my boys, although he is no boy anymore. What a sad story. He told me of his youthful dreams. And how many of his dreams are broken. He's had a rough twenty years. It breaks my heart to see a man whose heart is suffering. There's no way of recouping the lost twenty years. We cried together and we prayed together. But those years are gone, never to return. The saddest words of tongue or pen are these: "It might have been."

One day on the car radio I heard one of those songs about the old days—about the fifties. It was called, "The Class of '57 Had Its Dreams." Somehow that song got to me. The implication was that a lot of graduates' teenage dreams were shattered forever. When the whole class got together for a class reunion and looked at each other, they were a bunch of wrecks. For most, their high school graduation dreams hadn't come true. That's sad.

It doesn't have to be. There's hope. That's the beautiful thing about the gospel. It simply doesn't have to happen to you. Even if your father and mother divorce, people betray you, or your dreams of success fall flat, there's still hope!

The Lord said, "Oh that you had hearkened to my commandments. Your peace would have been like a river." He's saying, "Why are you so blind? I have shown you the way to go and you brazenly break with it, and you think you're going to get away with it? How foolish can you be?"

There are millions and millions who were brought up on the Bible, in Sunday school every Sunday, but today they are paying dearly for wasted years. The tears, the confessions, the crying, the sympathizing, the counseling never bring back the years they've lost.

All of us have relatives or friends who, after years of alcoholism, immorality, or some other form of sinful living, discover they've wasted the very best portion of their lives. Perhaps they finally come, brokenhearted, to Christ, truly repentant. Spiritually, they are new creatures. But physically, mentally, and psychologically, they and their families have scars that may take years, if ever, to erase.

I'll never forget sitting by the bedside of a young man who had been fatally injured in an accident. From what we could learn, he had never received Christ as his Savior. His father, who had wasted so many years in sinful, selfish pursuits, sat beside me humbly, saying over and over, "Luis, you can't go back. You just can't go back."

For the living, however, it's never too late, never too late to come back to the Lord, never too late to start over again. The Lord says in Romans 2:4, "Do you show contempt for the riches of his kindness, tolerance and patience, not realizing that God's kindness leads you toward repentance?"

The Lord may let you go a long way. It may seem that He is giving you endless rope. Why? Because He wants you to repent. He loves you so much. Come back to the Lord if you've been away from Him. Do not go on another day far from your Father in heaven. He is calling you back.

### Jacob tries to bargain
Genesis 28:18–22 (TLB) reads:

> The next morning he got up very early. He took the stone he had used as a pillow and set it upright as a memorial pillar. Then he poured olive oil over it. He named the place Bethel—"house of God"—though the name of the nearby village was Luz.
>
> Then Jacob made this vow: "If God will be with me and protect me on this journey and give me food and clothing, and if he will bring me back safely to my father, then I will make the LORD my God. This memorial pillar will become a place for worshiping God, and I will give God a tenth of everything he gives me."

What a vow! Who in the world asked him to make a vow in the first place? "*If* God will be with me and *if* He will keep me in this way that I go, and *if* He will give me bread to eat and clothing to wear, *so that* I come again to my father's house in peace, *then* the Lord shall be my God."

And to show that he was really nice, good old Jake said he would build a house right on the stone where he poured some oil. Further, he promised to give God ten percent of his profits.

He was something else! Incredible! This Jacob actually has the audacity to turn to God and say, "Hey, Lord, have I got a contract for you. It's a real beauty! It has only five points and it's very clear. Not thirty-five volumes. Just simple; clear. All you have to do is fulfill these five points, Lord, and then you can't imagine what a nice servant you're going to have on your hands. You'll be really proud to have me!"

Lots of people play that game with the Lord. If God prospers me—if I get good grades in high school—if this business deal goes through—if everything goes my way—one of these days, I'm going back to Sunday school. That must make the Lord feel great! Wasn't Jake being "very spiritual"? What a fantastic promise he made, right? The question is, whoever asked him to make that promise?

We must realize who God is. All Jacob thought about in that deal with God (which, by the way, was a total waste of breath) was food, clothing, protection, and territory. He didn't even mention God's purpose. That was far from his thinking. Jacob, only Jacob, was on his mind as he dared to bargain with God.

Years later, on a parallel occasion, when dealing with another "bargainer," Saul, God spoke these words: "To obey is better than sacrifice, and to heed is better than the fat of rams. For rebellion is like the sin of divination, and arrogance like the evil of idolatry" (1 Samuel 15:22–23).

When you cover up one sin, confusion sets in. Jacob wasn't thinking straight. He forgot to whom he was talking. Sin, not dealt with, always blinds us to God. What are you covering up? Are you trying to make a "deal" with the Lord? You're wasting your time. You don't realize how confused your thought processes are. Maybe it has become a habitual thing with you.

What a glaring contrast with another—who happened to be God's very own Son. He said, "I have come to do your will, O God" (Hebrews 10:7).

And of Him, Scripture states that Christ Jesus "made himself nothing, taking the very nature of a servant, being made in human likeness. And being found in appearance as a man, he humbled himself and became obedient to death—even death on a cross! Therefore God exalted him to the highest place and gave him the name that is above every name" (Philippians 2:7–9).

Jacob and Rebekah tried to cover up their sins with a bunch of good-sounding ideas. "Jacob, you go on over to your uncle's and marry a nice girl." Why should he marry a nice girl? He's a big crook. Why would any girl even want this Jake? He's a mafia-like character and now he tries to cover his past by marrying a "nice girl."

You don't make deals with the Lord. He initiates them with you. His plans are better, so much better than ours. His plans are perfect for us. But we're so stubborn. Don't waste the best years of your life. If God has His hand on you, He'll never let you go. "He who began a good work in you will carry it on to completion until the day of Christ Jesus" (Philippians 1:6). He'll do it! But what if you act stubbornly, if you don't follow His desire? He'll still bring it to completion, but you'll pay dearly for your stubbornness. It will hurt and it could be a very long hurting period.

However, here is that living possibility: "If we confess our sins, he is faithful and just and will forgive us our sins and purify us from all unrighteousness" (1 John 1:9). That is the patience of God. That is also the provision of God for the sins of His children. He is, after all, "the God of Jacob," as He often states.

### Quit trying to write your own contract

Many people today read the words, "In Christ all the fullness of the Deity lives in bodily form, and you have been given fullness in Christ, who is the head over every power and authority" (Colossians 2:9–10). Yet they keep groveling and begging and tramping around, looking for what they already have.

Instead of saying, "Thank you, Father, that in Jesus Christ dwells the whole fullness of God; and, because Christ is God 100 percent and because Christ lives in me, I am complete in Christ," you see them chasing around all over the place looking for "a blessing." That is insulting to God.

In Christ you *have* every single thing God ever planned for you and me. Everything? To go around looking for a different experience—an experience whose characteristics we outline for God to follow—is a blasphemous insult in the face of God Himself. It's "pulling a Jacob" on the Lord. It's whipping out a contract and saying, "God, if you'll give me this gift and that gift or if you'll provide thus and such, and if, then, I feel this and that way and speak this or that way, *then* I'll witness for you and serve you and be faithful to you. You'll see what a great club we'll form. Now do it, Lord."

That's making a deal with God! Scripture says, "Everything that there is of God is in Christ and you have come to fullness of life in Him." Everything we need, we have in Christ. By going around groveling and begging and searching, you're saying to God, "I don't really care about your contract, I want to write my own." Thousands of Christians live empty, unsatisfied lives because they have rejected God's offer, which is marvelous, perfect, complete! They insist on writing their own contract.

Is that you? If it is, confess it to the Lord and say, "Lord, forgive me. I've been childish. I've been acting from the flesh. Like Jacob did. But no more. I want to thank you that your blessed Son lives in me. In Him I've got everything I will ever need. Thank you."

Have you made the discovery that Christ lives in you? Not just as a doctrinal fact, but as living reality? Have you thanked Him for living in you? Have you thanked Him because everything He is, is yours? Or let me go a step back and ask you, have you ever actually received Jesus Christ into your life? Maybe you know a lot of doctrine, but you never *received* Him. If you have not, then that's why you're empty and confused. Open your heart to Him. By a simple prayer, trust Him. But if you have already received Christ, stop desperately searching around, looking for something you already have. Thank Him for what He has done. Theodore Monet, a Frenchman, penned these words:

O the bitter shame and sorrow
that a time could ever be
when I proudly said to Jesus,
"All of self, and none of Thee."

Yet He found me, I beheld Him,
bleeding on the accursed tree,
And my wistful heart said faintly,
"Some of self, and some of Thee."

Day by day His tender mercy,
healing, helping, full and free,
Brought me lower while I whispered,
"Less of self, and more of Thee."

Higher than the highest heavens,
Deeper than the deepest sea,
"Lord, at last Thy love has conquered,
None of self, and all of Thee."

# Chapter 3

# A Schemer to the End

*The God of Jacob*—the God we know, whom Jesus Christ revealed, is not only a sovereign God, a faithful God, a patient God and a God of government—He is also a God of judgment. God is a judge—a very strict, honest judge. You can't buy Him off. God is the kind of judge you can't bribe under any circumstances. He is a God of love, but also a God of judgment.

We recognize this as He now begins His heavy-handed work on this man, Jacob. It seems as if God gave Jacob all the rope he wanted. He let him go, go, go. Where is the Lord, you've been wondering? Well, it's His turn now. He is determined to mold and transform Jacob, to use the New Testament revelation, to conform him "to the likeness of his Son" (Romans 8:29).

Jacob sped on his way and soon arrived at his Uncle Laban's who welcomed him with open arms and immediately made him one of the family. Then, when Jacob had been there about a month, clever Uncle Laban, who knew a good thing when he saw it, offered Jacob a deal, apparently allowing Jacob to name the terms. Genesis 29:15–30 (NLT) reads:

> Laban said to him, "You shouldn't work for me without pay just because we are relatives. How much do you want?"
>
> Now Laban had two daughters: Leah, who was the oldest, and her younger sister, Rachel. Leah had pretty eyes, but Rachel was beautiful in every way, with a lovely face and shapely figure. Since Jacob was in love with Rachel, he told her father, "I'll work for you seven years if you'll give me Rachel, your younger daughter, as my wife."
>
> "Agreed!" Laban replied. "I'd rather give her to you than to someone outside the family."
>
> So Jacob spent the next seven years working to pay for Rachel. But his love for her was so strong that it seemed to him but a few days. Finally, the time came for him to marry her. "I have fulfilled my contract," Jacob said to Laban. "Now give me my wife so we can be married."
>
> So Laban invited everyone in the neighborhood to celebrate with Jacob at a wedding feast. That night, when it was dark, Laban took Leah to Jacob, and he slept with her. And Laban gave Leah a servant, Zilpah, to be her maid.
>
> But when Jacob woke up in the morning—it was Leah! "What sort of a trick is this?" Jacob raged at Laban. "I worked seven years for Rachel. What do you mean by this trickery?"
>
> "It's not our custom to marry off a younger daughter ahead of the firstborn," Laban replied. "Wait until the bridal week is over, and you can have Rachel, too—that is, if you promise to work another seven years for me."
>
> So Jacob agreed to work seven more years. A week after Jacob had married Leah, Laban gave him Rachel,

too. And Laban gave Rachel a servant, Bilhah, to be her maid. So Jacob slept with Rachel, too, and he loved her more than Leah. He then stayed and worked the additional seven years.

## The same old Jacob

Jacob's self-confidence seemed to be limitless. He seemed to have an incredible, obnoxious amount of self-confidence. With his mouth and his brains he felt he would work his way out of anything and get anything he wanted. He was a bargainer from the word *go*.

So all this time Jacob was getting into deeper trouble, as far as the Lord was concerned. But his sinful self-confidence was so enormous that it blinded him to himself. And his blindness and that self-confidence were proportionate. Jacob would have been a positive-thinker's case study delight.

Many of us operate in the same way. When I first came to the United States, the Lord used Ray C. Stedman in my life to deal with me very strongly. It wasn't the last blow I needed, but it was a big step.

That summer I served as one of Ray's first pastoral interns, along with Charles Swindoll. Ray knew there was something in my life I needed to settle. We sat down in his office and he told me I had to settle this matter now—and settle it right. But very self-confidently I said, "Oh, don't worry. I'll just write a letter. Then, when I get back to Argentina, I'll talk to them all. It's no problem. I'll fix it up. I'll just talk to them and it will all be over. I can just keep going forward."

Ray put his arm around me and quietly said, "You know, Luis, you think that you can get out of anything, don't you? One of these days, with that tongue of yours, you are going to dig yourself a hole and bury yourself so deep that nobody will be able to get you out of it. Not even God."

Was I really that bad? He went on, still with his arm around me.

"You know something else, Luis? You are so cocky. So proud. It seeps out of your pores and you don't even realize it. You came up to the States with a black suit and a black tie—to prove your spirituality. You think you're really something else."

He went on and on. I felt like saying, "Stop!" But I knew he was telling the truth. How it shook me! It was the beginning of a great awakening in my life.

### One of God's favorites

Jacob was this kind of man, blinded by his confidence in his own natural abilities. But no matter how self-confident you may be, the judgment of God goes on. You can't play games with God. You may think you can—all of us do, until God touches us and breaks us. Somehow we feel we're God's favorite children and we can get away with things that other people obviously cannot and should not.

The devil, of course, promotes this by whispering in our ear, "Hey, it's all right. You're one of God's favorite boys. It's all right. He'll let you get away with a little more carelessness, playing with little sins, a little fooling around. Don't worry. You've been doing it for years and nothing's happened. No car has run into you; your money is still coming in. Go on. It's going to be all r-i-i-i-ght."

Because Jacob got away with it for so long, he forgot that God is a God of judgment. You may be playing games with God in some area of your life and God seems to be giving you endless rope.

"I'm going to get away with it," you tell yourself. "I always have."

But you're not! Eventually the time of reckoning comes.

In Galatians 6:7–8, we read: "Do not be deceived: God cannot be mocked. A man reaps what he sows. The one who sows to please his sinful nature, from that nature will reap destruction; the one who sows to please the Spirit, from the Spirit will reap eternal life."

Jesus loves you, certainly. But Jesus is also the judge. Not only a judge the day we meet Him at the judgment seat of Christ, He is the judge now. He is at work in our lives in such a way that He is judging us now, in discipline and in correction for our growth to "conform us to the image of His Son."

I had a good friend in Argentina. When we were seventeen, we started out seriously serving the Lord. We were baptized at approximately the same time. He was the one who taught me how to preach in the streets. He taught me how to gain people's attention in the open air. I was a terrible public speaker—but if I've learned to capture people's attention, I owe it in some measure to him.

He was a great musician. He had an appealing personality. He was the life of the party. He could sell Bibles better than anybody I've ever seen. He taught me so much.

But one day when he was twenty-one, he went to another city. He had a physical problem and went to see a doctor. This doctor told him that his problem was due in part to the fact that he had been chaste. He prescribed a sex experience for my friend. Then my friend, despite knowing full well what Scripture has to say about such acts, followed the advice of this physician and committed an immoral act.

I didn't know anything about all this. One day I met him on the street. I noticed something completely different on his face. Something happens, you know, when a person commits immorality. Something leaves that never comes back. The glow is gone; it leaves scars. I noticed it right away.

"Juan," I said, "what in the world's happened to you?"

He told me the whole story. But he added, "Don't worry. I'll recuperate. I'll get up early in the morning and start reading the Bible and praying as we did in the old days, remember? It's going to be all right. Don't worry about me."

Twenty years later he was doing nothing for the Lord.

Then I heard about a man I've known for many years, a minister, a graduate of one of the best universities in the southwestern United States and of one of the best seminaries in the land. He had attended some of the best training courses and pastored great churches with good elders and staff. Yet he obtained a divorce.

Divorce doesn't happen overnight. A person doesn't go to a judge and say, "I'm getting along so well with my wife, Sue, but I'm going to divorce her tomorrow." It builds over a long time. Most of the time, immorality is involved. I'm convinced of that because I counsel hundreds of people around the world.

Now I don't know when or how the problem started with my friend. Maybe he thought he could get away with something because he was a pastor. I don't know if he's resigned his church yet. Obviously he or his wife thought they were getting away with it.

But no one gets away with sin. You and I have to realize that we cannot play games with God. In this superficial new terminology that we have allowed to seep into our lives and churches, we now want to talk about only the positive. We ignore the fact that so much tragedy is going on around us. When we see it, we wonder why. Why? Because somewhere, someone's covering up sin, that's why; and we won't discuss it by name.

### Jacob meets his equal

That's exactly what Jacob was doing. Trying to gloss over and forget his sinful past. God allowed Jacob to meet his match in his sly, tricky equal—his Uncle Laban. They were two of a kind. It's a toss-up who was the worse of the two. They wheeled-and-dealed over two basic issues. One, marriage. The old dad wanted to see his two daughters well cared for and he saw this wise, enterprising young man as a good catch. So he found a way to attach both of his daughters to him.

They also got to bargaining over big business (Genesis 30:25–43). Each of them was trying to outdo the other. It's so funny to read about. I recommend you read the whole story (Genesis chapters 29–30).

The sad thing is this. Jacob went on that journey, not only fleeing Esau, but going, so he thought, to marry a nice girl. But because he was out of step with God, he didn't marry a nice girl. He married a good-looking girl, evidently, but not a good one.

Her father was involved in spiritism. Genesis 30:27 (NLT) says:

> "Please don't leave me," Laban replied, "for I have
> learned by divination that the LORD has blessed me
> because you are here."

The father was a spiritist—or a liar. And not only
that, but both the father and the daughters, including the
beloved Rachel, were idolators. Genesis 31:19–20 reports
that "when Laban had gone to shear his sheep, Rachel
stole her father's household gods. Moreover, Jacob
deceived Laban the Aramean . . . . "

Then in Genesis 31:34–35 (NLT) we read:

> Rachel had taken the household gods and had stuffed
> them into her camel saddle, and now she was sitting on
> them. So although Laban searched all the tents, he couldn't
> find them. "Forgive me for not getting up, Father," Rachel
> explained. "I'm having my monthly period." So despite his
> thorough search, Laban didn't find them.

Rachel was obviously not above fabricating deceit;
lying to her own father, who was looking for his favorite
god. They were having a hassle over their idols; and
Rachel got away with the theft. So, Jacob didn't marry a
nice girl. Being out of God's will, he married a spiritist
who worshiped idols.

We can learn from this a lesson that sometimes
needs to be emphasized. Proverbs 4:19 says, "The way of
the wicked is like deep darkness; they do not know what
makes them stumble." Isn't that the truth?

Two professors from a state university came for
counseling during a crusade on the west coast of
America, and similar people came from the professions,
from big business—important people. They were stumbling over many issues and didn't always realize what

they were stumbling over! The way of transgressors is hard.

Poor old Jacob was being defrauded on all sides. He was being deceived in marriage, in business, and in every possible way. He wasted twenty years of his life because he refused to submit to God.

### All that scheming—for what?

Jacob kept playing by Laban's rules, still thinking he had to work out God's purposes by his own efforts. Apart from wheeling and dealing over a marriage, Jacob began dabbling in big business. He and Laban went back and forth. Who was going to keep the lambs? Who was going to keep the cows? The sheep? Everything. They hassled each other back and forth and finally they both became rich. Actually, the Lord worked it out so that each ended up with about equal portions anyway.

It's a pity Jacob went through all the cheating and all the shady business deals that he pulled on his uncle, because just a short time later he lost it all. When the famine took over the land, it took everything he had. Clinging to human comforts, possessions and wealth, we may unconsciously slide into shady business deals— maybe not big deals, but little deals, just to be more secure. We would do so much better to cling to the Lord.

A beautiful passage in Psalm 34 reads: "Taste and see that the LORD is good; blessed is the man who takes refuge in him."

If only Jacob had taken refuge in the Lord and said, "Lord, Laban can have all his sheep and his goats and his cows and his horses; I'm going back to where I belong. Lord, you provide." He could have been a happier man.

God is judging Jacob. He is getting, as they say in Britain, "tit for tat." Every shady deal he pulled on his brother, Esau, his uncle was pulling on him. On top of all that, now he has to go home and face Esau all over again.

# Chapter 4

# Jacob's "Reality Therapy"

### Oh-oh! Here He Comes!

Jacob prepares to face his original "enemy." He is being forced to settle his affairs. Genesis 32:1–5 (NLT) reads:

> As Jacob and his household started on their way again, angels of God came to meet him. When Jacob saw them, he exclaimed, "This is God's camp!" So he named the place Mahanaim.
>
> Jacob now sent messengers to his brother, Esau, in Edom, the land of Seir. He told them, "Give this message to my master Esau: 'Humble greetings from your servant Jacob! I have been living with Uncle Laban until recently, and now I own oxen, donkeys, sheep, goats, and many servants, both men and women. I have sent these messengers to inform you of my coming, hoping that you will be friendly to us."

The messengers returned with the news that Esau was on his way to meet Jacob—with an army of four hundred men! Jacob was terrified at the news. He divided his household, along with the flocks and herds and camels, into two camps. He thought, "If Esau attacks one group, perhaps the other can escape."

Still scheming and planning. Still the old Jacob. And what a treacherous deed he is about to commit. To save his own skin, he is willing to sacrifice his servants. How low can a man sink? Yet, that's what happens when someone strays from walking in the light with God.

Genesis 32:9–14 reads:

> Then Jacob prayed, "O God of my grandfather Abraham and my father, Isaac—O LORD, you told me to return to my land and to my relatives, and you promised to treat me kindly. I am not worthy of all the faithfulness and unfailing love you have shown to me, your servant. When I left home, I owned nothing except a walking stick, and now my household fills two camps! O LORD, please rescue me from my brother, Esau. I am afraid that he is coming to kill me, along with my wives and children. But you promised to treat me kindly and to multiply my descendants until they become as numerous as the sands along the seashore—too many to count."
>
> Jacob stayed where he was for the night and prepared a present for Esau: two hundred female goats, twenty male goats, two hundred ewes . . . ."

### All right, Jacob, that's far enough!

This is it. Jacob is nearing rock bottom in his walking away from God, but from here on it's going to be uphill. There will be a dip here and there, but from this point on the Lord has His way—visibly—with Jacob.

"Jacob, that's far enough!" the Lord seems to be saying. "I've given you all this leeway and you've gotten worse and worse, sinking deeper and deeper. Now I'm going to do a significant work in your life.

"The first step is that you are going to have to come back and walk in the light. To do that you must settle that sin that set you off on the wrong path years ago. You are going to have to face Esau."

Have you been straying from the Lord? Was it a year ago, ten years ago, or thirty years ago? (You remember well—it is something you can never forget.) You stepped out of God's will for your life. From that time on, it's been nothing but trouble and problems for you. You've gone away from the Lord; you've "cooled off" spiritually, and you keep saying to yourself and everyone else, "Why does the Lord allow this or that to happen to me?" You know full well why the Lord allows it. The Holy Spirit will not allow you to forget.

The Lord is saying, "Look, if you want to start walking in the light again, you must face that first sin that you committed. You must come out and face it in the light."

To Ephesus, the Lord Jesus said: "Remember the height from which you have fallen! Repent and do the things you did at first. If you do not repent, I will come to you and remove your lampstand from its place" (Revelation 2:5).

We need to keep in mind that God judges us and brings us to repentance for good reasons—one, for the vindication of His name, and two, for our welfare. Hebrews 12:11 says, "No discipline seems pleasant at the time, but painful. Later on, however, it produces a harvest of righteousness and peace for those who have been trained by it."

Scripture also says, "If we walk in the light, as he is in the light, we have fellowship with one another, and the blood of Jesus, his Son, purifies us from all sin" (1 John 1:7).

Face that sin; confess it. Then the blood of Christ can cleanse you and you can continue walking in the light. God can begin to fulfill His purposes in your life. For God to fulfill the purposes He declared years earlier—in and through Jacob, Jacob has to face up to his sin.

You and I who know Jesus Christ, if we step out of His will and His way—no matter if that misstep happened thirty years ago—will find that God will help us face that sin and clear it up. Then we can, once again, be walking in His will. Because God is God and He will fulfill His purposes.

### His purposes shall be true
In Isaiah we read, in chapter 46, verses 9–11:

> Remember the former things, those of long ago; I am God, and there is no other; I am God, and there is none like me. I make known the end from the beginning, from ancient times, what is still to come. I say: My purpose will stand, and I will do all that I please. From the east I summon a bird of prey; from a far-off land, a man to fulfill my purpose. What I have said, that will I bring about; what I have planned, that will I do.

Now when God determines to do something through your life (and He purposes to do something through every Christian's life), He's going to do it! The longer we resist, the farther it will be to go back to the place where we stepped out of His will.

### I'm with you
God revealed to Jacob that He had provided for him an invisible, protective care. Genesis 32:1–2: "Angels of God met him. When Jacob saw them, he said, 'This is the camp of God!' So he named that place Mahanaim."

God in His grace tells Jacob, "Look, Jacob, you are going to have to face up to your sin—you're going to have to clear things up with your brother. He knows you've hurt him. You've got to get his forgiveness. But listen, I've got an army on your side. Don't panic. I'm with you, even in your repentance. I'm surrounding you with an army of angels." The Lord opened Jacob's spiritual eyes, so to speak, just as He did with another prophet later on. He tells Jacob, "I know you've gone far away from me, but I want you back so much that I've got all my hosts at the ready here to protect you, to keep you, to help you. Don't worry." God is actually looking forward to this day of reckoning and cleansing. After all, it signals a new beginning for this man He loves so deeply.

Properly impressed and awed, Jacob recognizes it and exclaims, "This is God's army!"

God may be pointing out something to you that you must settle and you're trembling just thinking about it. "I can't do it," you cringe; "I can't face up to it." Never forget that God is your Father. He is on your side. Look how He reassures Jacob . . . .

"Certainly it's dangerous to face your brother. Of course, you're afraid of him. You deceived and cheated him badly. But my whole army is behind you—forward march!"

Remember Psalm 34:7: "The angel of the LORD encamps around those who fear him, and he delivers them."

And that other Scripture, Hebrews 1:14: "Are not all angels ministering spirits sent to serve those who will inherit salvation?"

What big step do you have to take? Is it something you must settle that makes you feel weak just to think of it? You can't sleep at night? Listen, all that God has is at your disposal, because God loves you as a father. In Jeremiah 31:3 He says: " I have loved you with an everlasting love; I have drawn you with loving-kindness.'"

All His armies are with you to help you, strengthen you, and protect you. So go back and face that first enemy. Go to the place where you failed. The Lord is with you. He is eager to help you settle the problem and get you back in the light. But remember, confess in public only the sin that concerns the public. Confess to your Esau what has hurt Esau. When no one knows about your sin and no one but yourself, your body, your life, your future is affected, confess only to God. Misplaced confession can sometimes hurt worse than the sin.

> "Do not fear, for I am with you; do not be dismayed, for I am your God. I will strengthen you and help you; I will uphold you with my righteous right hand" (Isaiah 41:10).

Poor old Jacob. Remember, twenty years earlier Jacob fled because Esau had said, "I'm going to get that brother of mine. I'm going to kill him!" Those words rang in Jacob's ears. He is terrified now at the thought of facing Esau.

When we have to face up to responsibility for sins committed, we also fear, don't we? Any normal person does. I did. Years ago, I had certain things I had to make right. Big things that were quite important. It was a frightening experience. Yet I knew if I failed to settle it, my life would be worthless from that day forward. God could never have used me again. Thank God, He strengthened me and I did the right thing. Now I can walk the earth free in Jesus Christ.

### Yes, Lord, I see your army,
### but I've got this plan . . .

Strangely, even though God revealed to Jacob that the armies of God were with him, Jacob, the old schemer, is still plotting. "In great fear and distress Jacob divided the people who were with him into two groups, and the flocks and herds and camels as well" (Genesis 32:7).

In verse 2, Jacob named the place "Mahanaim." Mahanaim means "two armies." Jacob realized that there were really two armies—his own little army, but more important, the army of God. The lesson here? Self-confidence blinds us to God's provision. Jacob couldn't trust God, so he divided his own army into two parts. Once again the old schemer, even though he had a straight revelation from God that he would be protected, cannot—will not—trust God to work it out.

You and I have done that too, haven't we? We have a real problem and we bring it up to the Lord. We pray and yet, when we finish praying, we begin scheming all over again how to solve it on our own. We begin thinking of arguments, trying to find a way in the flesh—in the natural man—to settle the problem.

But then, at last, for the first time, Jacob prays in humility. This is actually the first time he's prayed in the whole passage. It's a very humble prayer. Even then, however, he starts exaggerating, trying to marshal arguments to convince the Lord and still trying to make a deal with the Lord.

Verse 11: "Save me, I pray, from the hand of my brother Esau, for I am afraid he will come and attack me, and also the mothers with their children. But you have said . . . . " [he's trying to convince the Lord to protect him.] "Lord, he's coming to butcher us all. He's a criminal. You know him, Lord. It's not just me he's after, it's these women and little children . . . ."

He really gets carried away, doesn't he? Why is it? Because his conscience is so guilty that exaggeration is his way of protection. That's the way it always is. It was part of his lifestyle to use exaggeration and heavy argumentation to prove his point.

Then at last the Lord does something with him. Genesis 33:1–3 (NLT) reads:

> Then, in the distance, Jacob saw Esau coming with his four hundred men. Jacob now arranged his family into a column, with his two concubines and their children at the front, Leah and her children next, and Rachel and Joseph last. Then Jacob went on ahead. As he approached his brother, he bowed low seven times before him.

Jacob didn't go in front of the whole army, only before the women and the children. Sort of a repelling sight, isn't it? Jacob "eating dirt" as Americans say. "He himself went on ahead and bowed down to the ground seven times," Scripture describes it. But first of all, he is sending all his servants on ahead.

I love the Lord's irony here. After all the days and nights of Jacob's anguish—all the worrying, the scheming, the planning, and the organizing—what a big waste of time! Look at verses 4–10 (NLT):

> Then Esau ran to meet him and embraced him affectionately and kissed him. Both of them were in tears.
>
> Then Esau looked at the women and children and asked, "Who are these people with you?"
>
> "These are the children God has graciously given to me," Jacob replied. Then the concubines came forward

with their children and bowed low before him. Next Leah came with her children, and they bowed down. Finally, Rachel and Joseph came and made their bows.

"And what were all the flocks and herds I met as I came?" Esau asked.

Jacob replied, "They are gifts, my lord, to ensure your goodwill."

"Brother, I have plenty," Esau answered. "Keep what you have."

"No, please accept them," Jacob said, "for what a relief it is to see your friendly smile. It is like seeing the smile of God!"

Two things here. First, Jacob is really working over Esau's ego tremendously. Secondly, he is saying a terrible truth. The people we have wronged always represent God to us unless and until we settle real issues. To see the face of the person he has wronged put such fear into Jacob that it was like facing God in judgment. Yet it's ironic that he wasted so much time, energy, and sleepless nights planning, desperately trying to find a way to appease an Esau who needed no appeasement. For when they met, Esau threw his arms around him in greeting!

How many nights and days have you wasted foolishly scheming and planning in the flesh? How many years have you wasted? Why don't you come back to the Lord *right now* and simply say, "O God, what a fool I've been. How Jacob-like. It hasn't been worth it. Father, I'm coming back. I'm stripping myself of all the maneuvering and the scheming and the strategizing. Please cleanse me through the blood of my Lord Jesus Christ and, once and for all, let me walk again in the light." (Here may I recommend you read and meditate on 1 John, chapter 1, in the New Testament?)

God reveals Himself here as the Father. What a wonderful thing! He changed Esau's heart so that when he meets Jacob, instead of wanting to murder him, he simply hugs him.

Why don't you let God be God the Father in your life? "Your heavenly Father knows," our Lord Jesus states (Matthew 6:32). The Lord will prepare the way for you much like He did for Jacob. He has done it many times for me. He is willing and eager to do it for all of us.

If we were to ask Jacob after all these years, was it worth it? Was it worth all the scheming, the strategizing? Was it worth it, Jacob? He would answer as I have quoted before, "The years of my pilgrimage are a hundred and thirty. My years have been *few and difficult,* and they do not equal the years of the pilgrimage of my fathers" (Genesis 47:9, italics added).

How sad to end life that way. It doesn't have to be. Because God is a loving heavenly Father. His discipline and judgment are simply to bring you back into the light. He wants to love and care for you as a Father.

Don't play games anymore. Don't try to fool God. Let Him cleanse you through the blood of Christ and start you walking in the light. You'll be a free and happy man or woman, free to be the instrument of God's purposes in the world.

# Chapter 5

# The Liberating Climax

*What is your reason for living?* If you feel that living is simply going to work every morning and being bored at home every evening, you're mistaken. The purpose for living is to be an instrument for the fulfillment of God's purposes. This gives tremendous meaning to life. View your work—whether it's Christian work, a secular business, or housework—as part of the outworking of God's purposes in your life, in your family, and even in the world. For then you can see your part in the whole plan of God.

Before Jacob was even formed in his mother's womb, God had His hand on him. He spoke to Jacob and revealed Himself to him in his youth. But Jacob, like many of us, was a rebellious boy. He was a rebellious old man, too. At fifty he was tenaciously set in his pattern of resisting God's will. But God was bringing Jacob to a climax where He would break that old pattern. Jacob would start a completely new life, a life under the control of God.

### The moment of truth

For Jacob, unfortunately, his life had been one long struggle to this point. It was a self-produced struggle. He brought it on himself. Then he was cornered. Remember how he left his uncle, after stealing a lot of sheep and goods from him. He was running. Suddenly one night, just before he has to meet Esau, he realized the next morning is the moment of truth. Reality therapy is about to burst in upon him. He is so frightened he can't bear it. He thinks the end has come.

*Jacob, you're finished!* he tells himself. *You're dead, man. All your sure-fire schemes have come to nothing. Tomorrow you meet Esau.*

Under these circumstances, night finds Jacob all alone in the darkness of the desert.

Genesis 32:22–32 (NLT) reads:

> During the night Jacob got up and sent his two wives, two concubines, and eleven sons across the Jabbok River. After they were on the other side, he sent over all his possessions. This left Jacob all alone in the camp, and a man came and wrestled with him until dawn. When the man saw that he couldn't win the match, he struck Jacob's hip and knocked it out of joint at the socket. Then the man said, "Let me go, for it is dawn."
>
> But Jacob panted, "I will not let you go unless you bless me."
>
> "What is your name?" the man asked.
>
> He replied, "Jacob."
>
> "Your name will no longer be Jacob," the man told him. "It is now Israel, because you have struggled with both God and men and have won."

"What is your name?" Jacob asked him.

"Why do you ask?" the man replied. Then he blessed Jacob there.

Jacob named the place Peniel—"face of God"—for he said, "I have seen God face to face, yet my life has been spared." The sun rose as he left Peniel, and he was limping because of his hip. That is why even today the people of Israel don't eat meat from near the hip, in memory of what happened that night.

You may be wondering what all this business of thighs and sinew has to do with the eternal well-being of your soul! Actually it does. Note the next four points and then make a decision.

### A radical inner break

First, *Jacob experienced a desperate loss of hope.* This is the night before he meets Esau. He is convinced Esau is going to kill him. So as he lies there alone in the darkness, he says to himself, *I'm dead.* He feels in this moment the great crushing finality of his life.

All of us have to arrive at this point some time in our Christian life. If St. Paul did, how much more you and I must. If you and I are going to know the power of God in our lives, the power of Jesus Christ who indwells us by the Holy Spirit, there must come a time when we go through a tremendously critical experience, when suddenly we don't just settle isolated issues, but break completely with the old pattern and begin a fresh new pattern of living.

For St. Paul, this is how he expressed it (2 Corinthians 1:8–10):

> We do not want you to be uninformed, brothers, about the hardships we suffered in the province of Asia.

We were under great pressure, far beyond our ability to endure, so that we despaired even of life. Indeed, in our hearts we felt the sentence of death. But this happened that we might not rely on ourselves but on God, who raises the dead. He has delivered us from such a deadly peril, and he will deliver us. On him we have set our hope that he will continue to deliver us . . . .

My wife told me this turning point in her life came one summer when she was working as a counselor at a Christian camp. One of the main reasons she was there was to look for a marriageable man. Counseling was simply an interesting, acceptable sideline.

She was going through a real struggle. On the way to camp, she had stopped in northern California to visit a young man whom she thought was marriage-minded. That hadn't worked out.

All summer long as she counseled, her "antennae" were out, looking, looking. It didn't work. And in her soul she knew she had to quit scheming. She made the final decision to stop this foolishness, to stop trying to force God's hand and make a big mistake, potentially wrecking the rest of her life. So, she decided she would register at Multnomah School of the Bible in September, for she intended to become a missionary and leave the whole matter in God's hands.

That November, she and I came face to face. God had a plan all ready—for both of us. I'm so very thankful.

It's a tough decision to make. So many women and men have forced God's hand and married the wrong person, only to be heartbroken years later. How foolish and stubborn we are.

One of my key verses in life is Galatians 2:20: "I have been crucified with Christ and I no longer live, but

Christ lives in me. The life I live in the body, I live by faith in the Son of God, who loved me and gave himself for me."

I am crucified with Christ.

Have you come to that decisive moment in your life?

Have you, *by an act of your will,* accepted the fact that you are crucified with Christ? Or are you still trying to live the Christian life through self-effort? Are you still trying to enjoy life through actions stemming from self-will? Are you trying to solve your marriage problems on your own?

God wants to do something new and fresh and fantastic in your life. Some people think that a happy marriage is a marriage with no problems. That's not the point at all. All marriages have moments of turbulence. The secret lies in this—if Christ is in control and the Scriptures are lived out by the power of the indwelling Holy Spirit, we can overcome, love each other, and solve the problems through His power.

2 Corinthians 5:14–15 reads: "Christ's love compels us, because we are convinced that one died for all, and therefore all died. And he died for all, that those who live should no longer live for themselves but for him who died for them and was raised again."

## Wrestling with God

Second, *God comes down to wrestle Jacob into surrender.* Notice, Jacob was left alone that night. Each one of us has to settle with God, on a personal basis, alone. If you are a rebellious man, woman, young person, you have to settle your attitudes with God . . . alone.

The place where Jacob had this decisive surrender is called Peniel. Peniel means "the face of God." Jacob came face to face with God that night. You must also. Eventually, all of us must. And the sooner, the better.

The problem is yours. You must settle it. Alone with God. Say, "Oh God, I can't go on this way. I will not let you go (as Jacob said to God) until you bless me. I'll *not* let you go!"

You may feel you are having a wrestling match inside your soul with God. Maybe you feel like you're being torn apart. This is good! All of us need to come to the point where we feel exactly the way Jacob did that night. *I've had it. I'm dead! I've come to the end of my rope. I'm either going to kill myself . . . I'm going to get a divorce . . . I'm going to take some drastic action. I can't take any more.* The end of self-effort at last!

Some people experience a breakdown. Occasionally when things are tense, I say in jest to one of my team members, "I'm going to get on an airplane and have myself a breakdown on the way to the next crusade." The tension is so high. That's a standing joke with us. But for many people it is no joke. When they can't take it anymore, they fall apart. They see a psychiatrist. The answer is—to surrender. The purpose of wrestling, as I understand it, is to force a man down. Pin him down until he says, "I give up."

But the purpose of wrestling a man is to grab him, and by sheer force and technique throw him down, pin him until he can't move and says, "I give up." He surrenders. In a word, his struggle is over.

The interesting thing is that the one who came down to wrestle with Jacob was God Himself. What a sight in that lonesome desert night. Another interesting thing—Jacob is such a persistent rebel. He wrestled with God *all night.* That's quite a wrestling match! Finally, when the sun was coming up on the horizon, God said to Jacob, "All right, Jake, let go. The sun is coming up!"

## God vs. ego

What does this have to do with a victorious Christian life? Jacob shows us the very limits of rebellion against God. If God encountered you tonight and wanted to wrestle you down, would you say, "Lord, whatever you want, you can have it!"

Not Jacob. And truthfully, not many of us either. Some people wrestle with God all their lives. Some people feel that "wrestling with God" is a sign of spiritual sensitivity and deep spirituality. Actually, it is a sign of rebellion and obstinacy.

Haven't you heard people say, "I'm having a battle with God over an issue"? That is being "really spiritual," they think. A battle with God! It is an indication of their enormous ego.

I once asked Dr. Ray Stedman how, in his counseling, he broke through all the underbrush, the smokescreens, the facades that people throw up, even when in deep trouble. "How do you get to the point so quickly and discover the problem?"

"Luis," he said, "there's only one real problem in life. All the others are just an outgrowth of it, a smokescreen. It's the ego. Quickly find out who's in control of the ego and you know the source of everything."

I've practiced that on television. Some critics say, "Palau doesn't even listen. He goes on to answer problems before they finish life-details related to the question." It's because I follow that precept. Every problem a person has stems from an ego that is uncontrolled by Jesus Christ. You can cut through all the smokescreens and the masks and all the ways people try to impress you, and you'll discover their problem stems from a selfish ego. That's how it is with me. It is true of the human family.

### You've got to start limping

Jacob wouldn't give in. All night he wrestled with God. Then suddenly, "When the man saw that he could not overpower him, he touched the socket of Jacob's hip so that his hip was wrenched as he wrestled with the man" (Genesis 32:25). One touch from God put him out of joint. God saw that this was it. He had to teach Jacob a lesson. He touched the hollow of his thigh, putting it out of joint. Jacob became weak. The wrestling match was over.

The third point is submitting fully to God. The thigh muscle, probably the strongest muscle in the body, is a picture of *Jacob's point of greatest natural human strength*—the thing he always felt he could fall back on in times of trouble. Whenever Jacob was in trouble, what did he do? He ran away, didn't he? That was his solution to every problem. Run. He must have had tremendous legs. He'd probably be a great Olympic runner if he were living today. So the Lord may have said, "Okay, Jacob thinks when he meets Esau, perhaps in a moment of real human strength, he's going to turn and run away. I'm going to touch him so he can't run anymore."

All of us have some point where we feel we're really strong. Everyone. Yet St. Paul said in 2 Corinthians 12:10, "When I am weak, then I am strong." We don't like that truth. God has to allow us to corner ourselves. Then, when we have nowhere to run, He touches us.

From then on, Jacob limped. He limped the rest of his life—he could never walk straight. He couldn't run very fast. Never again could he escape from his situations by running. That threw him on God. He had to look up. He had to rely on God.

What is your point of great natural strength? Surrender it to God now. Come to Him, saying, "Oh, God, there is this thing in my life that I'm always glorying about"—whether secretly or publicly glorying.

What is it with you? For some people, it's their wits. They can outwit anybody in church. For some, it's a fast tongue. Any problem, leave it to them. They can handle it! Are you the kind of person who can talk people into things? You say, "Aw, don't worry, I'll settle it . . . I'll talk my wife into it . . . no sweat."

Maybe you're an operator with committees. "Just let me get a committee together and I'll fix it." And you talk to each one individually, railroad the issue, and have it your way. By the time they come to the committee meeting, you've convinced them and the vote goes the way you want. You go home, chuckling to yourself, *I can do it any time. Leave it to me.* Is that your point of strength?

Some people glory in their emotions. They've just come from a great time of worship with God. This is their glory. I have seen more people fall into immorality who were at one time glorying in a superlative thing *they* called "worship," because they think that the noise and the excitement was the worship. They concentrate on that and when temptation comes, the emotion also gets them. They go over the hill.

What is the strong point on which you rely whenever you're in trouble? There are the thinkers. Profound Christians. "I write poetry and great music. I meditate. I don't talk much, but I think." When there's trouble, they clam up. They settle problems by not talking about them, thinking that's their strength.

Whatever your stronghold of natural strength, God is going to touch it. He has to. By not relying on His power, you are depending on your natural strength. And God can't use you in that state. 2 Corinthians 12:9 says, "*My* power is made perfect in weakness" (italics added).

Have you about had it? You may feel, *I've just got to be free. I can't take another day, another week.* It may be your family situation and you're saying, "I want to start over again."

Is it a sex temptation that is haunting you? You may feel, *I'm about to fall.* It isn't enough to just confess it. A whole new pattern has to be set. You've got to start limping. You need to realize you *don't* have what it takes to live the Christian life. Only Jesus Christ does!

All of us must come to the point of crucifixion, to Jesus Christ, and say, "Oh God, I don't want to go the way of all flesh. I want to be a man or woman of God. I want to be holy. I want to be clean." There must be a radical inner break.

### The smell tells you it's garbage

It isn't enough to just settle the marriage issue or the sex temptation alone. The whole pattern of your life must change to "*I* no longer live, but Christ lives in me" (Galatians 2:20, italics added). That's the whole key.

It isn't that you surrender the sex temptation and then you surrender the lying problem. Then the fighting, etc. No, you come to Him and say, "Lord, touch me where I need it so that it will no longer be *I* trying to live the Christian life, not *I* trying to overcome temptation, but *you*, Lord Jesus. *You* living in me, having *your* way through my life, in my home and ministry and work."

We live in especially difficult days, particularly regarding the home situation and the sex temptation problem. You have to re-pattern if you've gotten into the habit of reading suggestive stimulating literature. That is something that can ruin a man's mind and his home. I'm not a prude. I'm not a fool or blind man—but almost every magazine today has at least one article that is suggestive or, worse, sexually explicit. Dangerous garbage! You don't have to climb into a garbage truck and wallow in it to know it's filled with garbage. The smell tells you right away. Yet, there are Christians who think reading this type of material "keeps them up with what is going on in the world" and they wallow in it. A dangerous game.

Listen, that's a satanic lie. I have talked to many couples who are going through troubles, and it all started with either the man or the woman consistently reading, filling their mind with moral, sexual, and spiritual pollution. Their minds have been infiltrated and intoxicated with suggestive and stimulating literature.

Most of us at one time or another have read something that paints the sex act twenty times bigger than it can or ever will be. You read about these "super" men who can do in one night what it would take a typical husband a month to do. But men read this and think something is wrong with their marriage. They fall into the belief that they are missing out on something. Actually, it's just a satanic scheme. The publishers of these articles are out to get your money and Satan is using them to wreck your home.

This may seem like an indelicate subject among decent Christians. But I'll tell you, it could wreck your home. Maybe some of you come from broken homes. You know, it could be that your dad left your mother and that it all began with his reading impure literature.

I often travel by air and have concluded that airport pocketbook racks are the world's biggest garbage pails. I've seen adult men, executive types, looking through these racks. They buy one, take it on the plane and sit with the cover turned because it's a filthy book. Then, when they walk out, they throw it in the garbage can. They wouldn't get caught reading it, but their minds are full of it.

Also, this philosophy that's being peddled about the joyous freedom of the single life. It's built up as one great big picnic. If only you could talk to those who pretend. They're the most miserable, lonely, empty, self-centered creatures you'll ever meet. But people swallow that story. Some of you have bought that lie and are about to break up your home. You blindly refuse to submit to God and Jesus Christ. You think you'll find freedom leaving your wife? You'll never be free! God tolerates divorce only on the basis of adultery.

Then there is another danger. They call it, "Games people play." Flirting. Even in so-called Christian circles. Men and women flirt with each other. Men make passes at each other's wives. And women allow it. This leads to the destruction of the spirit. You should not tolerate it in yourself or in the other person. If a man makes a pass at your wife, don't let him in your home again. He's not your friend. He's an enemy.

In certain circles it has become fashionable—it's okay. Well, it is *not!* God says, "You shall be holy for I am holy." Jesus Christ said, "Blessed are the pure in heart for they will see God" (Matthew 5:8). Hebrews 12:14

records, "Make every effort . . . to be holy; without holiness no one shall see the Lord." There are two meanings here. One: Without the robe of righteousness, which signifies that we are *in* Christ Jesus, we can never enter heaven and stand in the presence of the righteous God. And, two: Without holiness here, we lose the daily fellowship and communion with our loving Lord. We grieve Him. We lose the joy of His fresh anointing of us. We lose eye-contact with Him. We no longer enjoy His immediate, day-to-day companionship.

We are eternally *in* Him as believers when we accept Him as our Savior; but we can lose the profound joy of our salvation when we live unholy lives.

One summer, I was talking with a young man who said, "Luis, I just go crazy over women. I don't know how to overcome temptation." We spent a long time together and I told him how I overcome temptation. Several years later he came to me and told me, "You know, since talking with you I have had total victory over this problem and I thank you for telling me how you do it."

The first step to victory (and it's not just sex problems, but many other things) is to settle it deep in your soul as a new pattern of living. "God, I want to be holy. I know I won't be perfect, but holy I can be and will be. And I want Jesus Christ, the Son of God who lives in me, to make me the holy person I want to be. The person you want me to be.

"With your control, I *shall* overcome temptation and I *shall* overcome my old pattern of living. I will live on a completely different level because, Lord Jesus, you're going to have control over my life."

So God touched Jacob at the point of his natural strength, where Jacob thought he was big stuff, adequate plus, making him limp for the rest of his life. But from that time on, Jacob became tremendously powerful for God. God changed his name from Jacob, "the Grabber," to Israel, "One who prevails with God" (Genesis 35:9–10, TLB). The night of his wrestling match with God was the beginning of a new pattern for Jacob.

That's the way it happened to me, although I didn't wrestle with God that way. God met me at Multnomah Biblical Seminary in Portland, Oregon. I was finally able to understand at that point that it was not I but Christ living in me. Such a time must come for all of us, just as it did for Jacob.

## Change that lasts

Fourth, *after this, Jacob had a few ups and downs—but it was a completely new life.* He became a blessing to his sons. He was a blessing to the Pharaoh. He was fruitful, he multiplied; and through Joseph, he saw tremendous blessing come to the whole world. Jacob had a real transformation. It wasn't just that he changed his doctrine; his life was changed. Because from that moment on, he didn't rely on old Jacob's wiles and strengths; he came to rely on God. His life, his whole future was changed (Genesis 35:11–15).

There is a beautiful picture of Jacob as an old man. Joseph comes to him with his two sons, Jacob's grandchildren. Joseph falls prostrate on his face in front of Jacob and asks Jacob to bless his sons. Ancient old man Jacob, at the end of his life, puts his hands on the heads of these two little grandchildren and gives a fabulous blessing from God.

Look at Joseph, flat on his face (even though he was the virtual head of the Egyptian empire and of the whole world) because of his deep respect for Jacob, because his father was such a powerful man of God. Jacob would never have been this kind of man in his old age if God hadn't touched him, broken him, and become Lord of his life.

If you have been struggling and wrestling with God in your soul, I pray you will stop and say, "Oh, God, this is it. I want to die to the old way of living. I *am* crucified with Christ. It isn't I doing the living, but Christ, who lives in me. From here on, oh Lord, the life I live in the flesh, I will live trusting in the Son of God who loved me and gave Himself for me."

Don't wait until you are an old man or an old woman to take that step. Spend time alone with God—now. Tell him, "I don't understand everything; but whatever it is, that's what I want. I don't want to have terrible failures to weep over and beat my breast about when I'm old. I want to so live under the control of Jesus Christ that when I end my life I can look back on it and say, 'Lord, I have made mistakes, but praise your holy name, you were in control of my life.'"

Isn't that what you want?

"That's great for the kids," you say, "but I'm forty-five, and I've got some things in my past . . ." Put them under the blood of Jesus Christ. "The blood of Jesus, his Son, purifies us from all sin" (1 John 1:7). He will cleanse you and forget it. "Their sins and lawless acts I will remember no more" (Hebrews 10:17).

You *can* start again. You *can* be fruitful—a blessing to your children, to your grandchildren. In your old age you'll be a blessing to other people. If He's wrestling with you, surrender to Him. Tell Him, "Oh God, I'm glad to be pinned down. There's nowhere else I can go. Now take over."

And He *will* do it!

# *Interim Chapter*

*Well, that was Jacob's life*—130 years and most of it wasted as he "did his own thing." It is sad when you think of what might have been.

However, as we move on to study his son Joseph, we realize that it may have been Jacob's experiences and mistakes that made Joseph so sensitive to God, who chose and began to work in Joseph at a very early age. Joseph responded at once! What a difference from his father who balked every step of the way.

God began revealing Himself to Joseph through vivid, if sketchy, inner glimpses of his future. Through dreams and visions, Joseph began to see the ministry God had for him. I believe that God loves to speak to every one of us, through the Scripture, through a minister or a respected friend. His aim is to give us some hint of the usefulness He has for you and me who have accepted Jesus Christ as Savior and are now children of God, empowered by the indwelling Christ.

God chose Joseph, and Joseph knew it. Joseph simply responded to God. In responding, he became incredibly successful, to the glory of God. Have you responded to Him? He chose you and He called you.

Joseph faced four major life-changing crises. The first and possibly most shaking was being thrown into a pit at the hands of his own brothers, then sold as a slave for only twenty shekels.

Yet this admirable man, at the end of his years, could look back at his life and, specifically referring to that barbaric act, say to his brothers, "You intended to harm me, but God intended it for good" (Genesis 50:20). Yes, God had chosen Joseph. Joseph knew it; and he was successful because he trusted "the God who is there," to borrow Francis Schaeffer's phrase.

When God calls a man or a woman, it is because He has a plan for his or her life. He wants to do something. When he called you, elected you and saved you, He had a purpose and a complete plan in view. That's exciting! The Lord who called and appointed you wishes to speak to you, to remind you of an old promise or to give you a fresh word from Himself.

Look now at the life of Joseph, with a prayer that you will hear God speaking directly to you, telling you more about Himself, unfolding glimpses of His plan for your life in today's circumstances.

# Chapter 6

# Break and Run!

## The downhill plunge

Joseph's story begins with a downhill plunge. Because of Jacob's favoritism, in essence giving Joseph the birthright, Rachel's boy is envied and hated by his brothers. At their first opportunity, the brothers wreak revenge on him. The drama begins in Genesis 37:23–28 (NLT):

> When Joseph arrived, they pulled off his beautiful robe and threw him into the pit. This pit was normally used to store water, but it was empty at the time. Then, just as they were sitting down to eat, they noticed a caravan of camels in the distance coming toward them. It was a group of Ishmaelite traders taking spices, balm, and myrrh from Gilead to Egypt.
>
> Judah said to the others, "What can we gain by killing our brother? That would just give us a guilty conscience. Let's sell Joseph to those Ishmaelite traders. Let's not be responsible for his death; after all, he is our brother!" And his brothers agreed. So when the traders came by, his brothers pulled Joseph out of the pit and sold him for twenty pieces of silver, and the Ishmaelite traders took him along to Egypt.

However, the desperate plot takes a strange twist when Joseph arrives in Egypt because . . .

> The LORD was with Joseph and blessed him greatly as he served in the home of his Egyptian master. . . . Potiphar soon put Joseph in charge of his entire household and entrusted him with all his business dealings. From the day Joseph was put in charge, the LORD began to bless Potiphar for Joseph's sake. All his household affairs began to run smoothly, and his crops and livestock flourished. So Potiphar gave Joseph complete administrative responsibility over everything he owned. With Joseph there, he didn't have a worry in the world, except to decide what he wanted to eat! (Genesis 39:2–6 NLT).

We see the purposes of God worked out even in the intricate details of a young man's life. God in His sovereign will took hold of this teenager. He said, "Joseph, I am going to do something with you. You are really just a boy, but listen. You won't believe how I'm going to use you.

"For generations, Joseph, people are going to talk about you and learn from you. If you will walk with me like your fathers, Abraham, Isaac, and even Jacob (for with all his mistakes, your father still walks with me), you can't imagine how far I'm going to take you. Others may look at you as a young teenager; your brothers may laugh and say, 'Here comes the dreamer,' but I am going to use you."

God had allowed Joseph to be sold into slavery for twenty shekels, which was really nothing—thirty was the price of a slave. They just gave him away, but the Lord's hand was upon him. In the New Testament, Paul repeats this overwhelming idea; "No eye has seen, no ear has heard, no mind has conceived what God has prepared for those who love him" (1 Corinthians 2:9). It is amazing to see God so involved in the life of this teenager.

## God at every level

Now God has many things to deal with—the Egyptian empire, for instance, and the movement of His chosen people; yet His heart was set on this young man, Joseph.

That is one of the values of the Old Testament. In simple narratives, it reveals how smoothly, justly, and adequately God is working on several levels at the same time. He can be working with Pharaoh at a top political level; He can be working with old Jacob over here, with Jacob's sons over there, and with Joseph here. God is not restricted, as we are. He is omniscient, omnipotent and omnipresent. This divine ability is what theologians call "the government of God." Behind the curtain, He clearly governs historic events and the people who play their parts.

Today, He is working the same way. He is dealing with the president. He is dealing with the former Soviet Union, China, Israel, and India. He is working individually with you and with me.

An exciting thing about looking at the Old Testament is that you begin to understand why and how God can operate on all these levels simultaneously and still accomplish His purpose. In spite of distorted human behavior and even utilizing such behavior, whether it's a young teenager or the pharaoh, God is at work, using all these instances for His glory.

One sure sign that a person is rebellious in his heart against God and doesn't really accept the Bible's full

authority as God's Word is when he says, "I can't understand how God, in the Old Testament, could send the
Israelites to butcher all those men, women, and children
. . . I think that's terrible! How *could* God do that? I just
can't accept that."

When someone talks this way, he demonstrates
spiritual immaturity. Someone who is fighting God
refuses to look at the whole of revelation to see that God
is God. The answer is that God allowed those people to
be killed. He knows why He did it. Among other reasons, they were incorrigibly and criminally idolatrous.

God knows what He is doing. When God is working and operating on different levels, we can trust Him.
Never should we question incredulously what God does
or allows to happen in history or in our own lives.
Inquire, so as to understand His ways, yes. By all means.
But the unbelief that sneers at God's wisdom is dangerous ground on which to play.

We need to watch our approach to understanding
the purposes of God. We should say, "I do believe and
trust you. Now help me to understand your ways," not
"I cannot believe or understand. Now, you show me
why."

### The Lord was with him

Joseph was a successful slave. Genesis 39:2 says,
"The LORD was with Joseph and he prospered, and he
lived in the house of his Egyptian master."

Most of the commentaries I have read claim that his
master was probably Pharaoh's right-hand man, possibly the head of his personal bodyguard, which is always
an important position and in those days even more so.
Therefore, Joseph, slave though he was, actually sat

authoritatively close to one of the highest places of Egyptian government, and he was successful. What was his secret? Very simple: A God-centered person is a successful person—always.

Seven times in this chapter you read, "The LORD was with Joseph . . . the LORD was with him . . . the LORD gave him success in everything . . . the LORD blessed the household of the Egyptians . . . the blessing of the LORD was upon everything Potiphar had . . . the LORD was with him . . . the LORD was with Joseph and gave him success in whatever he did."

Who of us does not want to be successful and prosperous? I definitely do. And you can be by God's grace because the Lord is with you. The same is true with all of us. It is not the particular privilege of a few. You can become successful no matter what your present harassing circumstances may be. Never forget it. At this point Joseph was nothing but a slave, yet a successful one!

If you want to be a successful, prosperous person, the secret is the presence of the living God daily at work in your life. Is the Lord at work in your life? Or is the flesh at work? That is the important question. Joseph was successful because "the Lord was with him."

Someone might comment, "Well, the Lord is with all of us." Yes, but in the Scripture it means more than just the fact that the Lord is with everyone in a general sense. It means that the Lord was with Joseph in a particular way because Joseph was walking with the Lord. "If a man remains in me and I in him, he will bear much fruit" (John 15:5). There is a fundamental principle at work here. There must be an exchange. The Lord is with you and you respond to Him. Then it can be said, "The Lord is with that person. The Lord is at work in his life."

God was giving Joseph, a young man, success in the highest places of Egyptian life. God was training him and preparing him for the big job that He had for him more than ten years later.

Joseph, a slave in a foreign country, not knowing the language, could have been treated like a dog. But he was not. He climbed successfully. Isaiah 41:10 says, "Do not fear, for I am with you; do not be dismayed, for I am your God. I will strengthen you and help you; I will uphold you with my righteous right hand." That verse was not written in the days of Joseph, but the Lord proved the truth of this promise even then.

I don't know what has come into your life. Perhaps you are going through unexpected turmoil. Years ago, one of the members of our evangelistic team left, through no particular problem, simply because it was the Lord's will. Our team was still small in those days. This particular team member was a musician who helped us from time to time in the crusades. When we knew that the time was coming for him to leave, in my heart I was desperate. I could not imagine sitting on the platform without having this man, a great personal friend, there. I felt it was the end of our ministry. I paced up and down the hotel room where we were overseas. I felt so desperate inside. *We are finished as a team,* I thought.

Then, in doing my Bible memory work that week, I came upon Isaiah 41:10. I had to remind myself repeatedly, "Do not fear, for I am with you; do not be dismayed, for I am your God. I will strengthen you and help you; I will uphold you with my righteous right hand." Finally I had peace. And of course God has continued to pour out His blessings on our evangelistic team and through us in citywide and nationwide evangelism in scores of countries around the world.

Perhaps you are going through something like Joseph did. It may not be big. It could be small in other peoples' eyes; but for you it is insurmountable. The Lord says, "Fear not, for I am with you."

## Privilege put to the test

That was the secret of Joseph's success: the declared and very real presence of God and the blessing of God upon his life. As Joseph began to prosper, he might have thought, "At last I've beaten this slave thing. Now I'm in charge of this place. I'm going to stick it out. I'm general manager of the estate of one of the top men in the country. I'm going to play it cautiously and carefully. This is where I'm going to stay. My brothers thought they had me, but look at me now! The Lord has honored my faith."

Then suddenly when everything seems to be going right for him, a tremendous temptation comes his way. Genesis 39:6–15, 19 tells the account of how the wife of his master sought to tempt Joseph:

> Now Joseph was well-built and handsome, and after a while his master's wife took notice of Joseph and said, "Come to bed with me!"
>
> But he refused. "With me in charge," he told her, "my master does not concern himself with anything in the house; everything he owns he has entrusted to my care. No one is greater in this house than I am. My master has withheld nothing from me except you, because you are his wife. How then could I do such a wicked thing and sin against God?" And though she spoke to Joseph day after day, he refused to go to bed with her or even be with her.

One day he went into the house to attend to his duties, and none of the household servants was inside. She caught him by his cloak and said, "Come to bed with me!" But he left his cloak in her hand and ran out of the house.

When she saw that he had left his cloak in her hand and had run out of the house, she called her household servants. "Look," she said to them, "this Hebrew has been brought to us to make sport of us! He came in here to sleep with me, but I screamed. When he heard me scream for help, he left his cloak beside me and ran out of the house." . . .

When his master heard the story his wife told him, saying, "This is how your slave treated me," he burned with anger.

Joseph was "well-built and handsome." A sharp kid. We are all "well-built and handsome" to someone. But God was faithful and delivered Joseph out of this temptation, just as we can expect Him to provide a way of escape from temptation for us. There is that divine promise, nearly 2,000 years old and still solid, in 1 Corinthians 10:13 that says, "No temptation has seized you except what is common to man. And God is faithful; he will not let you be tempted beyond what you can bear. But when you are tempted, he will also provide a way out so that you can stand up under it."

As for the master's wife, let's consider several condemning descriptions of her character:

### Covetous

In the first place, she "took notice of" Joseph (verse 7). She began to covet him. Although covetousness begins in the heart, time and time again in Scripture the Lord emphasizes the part the eye plays. Covetousness begins, for many, with the eyes. The temptation begins from within, but the first thing noticed is that something that "catches the eye."

## Shameless

Secondly, she was shameless. She said, "Come to bed with me!" (verse 7). Passion, in contrast to love, is shameless. It may seem like great love; but outside of marriage, it is shameless.

## Persistent—accommodating

Thirdly, she was persistent. Day after day she pestered Joseph with her demands. Fourthly, she was accommodating. We read she wanted him "to go to bed with her or . . . be with her" (verse 10). She now understood that Joseph was not going to fall for an outright sexual temptation. Therefore, she suggested, in effect, "Well, if you are prudish and moralistic, just a little being together and keeping me company while my husband is on a trip can't hurt."

All the little flirtations that go on at parties—the indiscreet passes, the "casual" touching—are being accepted as normal. This occurs not only at cocktail parties. Men in the church make passes at women in the church, such as "Can I drive you home?" "How about a cup of coffee somewhere?" All sounding very innocent.

Men play two age-old tricks on women—all over the world—in this matter of immorality. With young girls, the old trick is where the boyfriend asks, "Do you love me?" She replies, "Yes." Then he asks her to prove it! Thousands of naive young girls have allowed themselves to fall into sexual immorality by that line of reasoning. And it keeps happening again and again. Even in our sophisticated age, young women still fall for it.

Many married women fall for the other sly trick in a moment of weakness. They meet an old high school friend at the store. He says, "Well, what do you know, Christine So-and-so! You don't look a year older than you did when we were in high school!" Are you kidding? After four kids and twenty years?

But someone with ulterior motives knows that this so often works. It appeals to a person's vanity. Many women actually believe such cheap lies. Something in the soul of men and women longs to believe such lies of Satan as, "Your husband has not mentioned your looks in years, Christine; but this old friend immediately does, even after twenty years. Could this be the true love you've been looking for so long?"

### Scheming

Then, in the fifth place, Potiphar's wife was a scheming woman. She finally found the right moment (Genesis 39:11–12), after probably waiting for months. She may even have worked it out so that there was no one there but the two of them. Then when they were quite alone, she went for him, grabbed his robe and hung on—a desperately passionate, egotistical woman.

It was not love, although even today passion is often peddled as love. So many homes are breaking up today, even among Christian believers. What are the causes? There are many causes, but very often this issue—scheming passion—is involved at some point, often as the final blow.

### "Love" turns on and off

Joseph faced up to it! This test helped Joseph really become the victorious young man God intended him to be. It is a satanic lie to believe that passion is equivalent to love, that because you become nervous, jittery, and "turned on" when you meet so-and-so that it is love, and that because "it is love" you have a natural right to the intimacy of sex. It is not love, and you do not have such a right!

Look at this proof: The moment Joseph rejected her, the so-called "love" became venomous hatred. Her passion became a desperate desire to destroy him. Many times that is what passion is—actual hatred or gross selfishness disguised as love, using the word "love" as an excuse.

## Joseph's defenses

Joseph effectively protected himself in several ways, and Scripture reveals these to us. In verse 8, "he refused." Joseph was virtually saying, "My spirit will not allow it." In the New Testament, Galatians 2:20 reminds us, "I have been crucified with Christ and I no longer live, but Christ lives in me."

## Refusal

"I am crucified!" Like Joseph, when faced with these matters of sexual temptation and flirting, I believe we must bring them to the foot of the cross, saying, "Lord Jesus, there is this thing. I would be a hypocrite or a fool to say it isn't present. I am being tempted. There are times when it comes to me, and this is one of those times. But, Lord, I want to settle this in my inner spirit. I want to refuse anything that has to do with playing with sex either mentally or physically, even a long-distance flirting. I want to deal with it thoroughly, radically, deeply."

All of us have to deal with this temptation. The sooner we do so, the better. Once it is settled, once the crucifixion has taken place, it does not mean that you will not be tempted anymore. But when the temptation comes again, the inner resolve that was obtained at the foot of the cross will make it easier to deal with it. Even though it may come in the most attractive and beautiful form, you can consider it settled—at the cross of Christ.

### Loyalty

Secondly, Joseph is saying, "I would be disloyal" (verses 8–9). "With me in charge," he told her, "my master does not concern himself with anything in the house; everything he owns he has entrusted to my care. No one is greater in this house than I am. My master has withheld nothing from me except you, because you are his wife."

### Reason

Thirdly, he says in effect, "You do not belong to me. You are *his* wife, not mine" (verse 9).

However, a single young man might argue about a single woman, "Sure she isn't my wife, but then she isn't anyone else's either. She is single." The Lord has one person for you, and she is the only one who belongs to you. And you belong to her. Therefore, this argument of Joseph's is also valid for two single people.

Intellectually, Joseph had settled the question. This is how God helps us overcome sexual temptation, by clarifying the problem in our mind. Certainly for us all there is the urge and sometimes the temptation, but intellectually you can settle it biblically. "She doesn't belong to me. He doesn't belong to me." Therefore, forget it.

## Honesty

Joseph cries out (in verse 9), "How then could I do such a wicked thing?" That word strikes home. Wickedness! Sexual relations outside of marriage are a great wickedness. It is not just "a little fooling around."

That is what is destroying the United States. If you think it is "just a little thing," go to Latin America and see what they are going through down there. Most of the countries are miserably poor. In some countries 70 percent of the population is illegitimate. There is a terrible nothingness in the structure of society in that part of the world because of sexual immorality.

I was brought up with such a high respect for the USA and all Protestant Anglo-Saxon nations because of their strong position on the family. However, I have come to realize that even in this country with all its education, its cultural development, its economic strength, the travel and the reading, there is much suffering and many problems in the area of sexual immorality.

One cannot say, "It is just a minor, secondary thing. You eat, you drink, you do it, you forget it." No, you do not forget it! Immorality is a great wickedness. Joseph recognized the fact that it is a sin against God. "Why should I sin against God?" Joseph must have been tremendously tempted, just like anyone else in the same situation would be. But he had settled it spiritually. He had settled it intellectually. He had settled it with the Lord. "It is wrong. It is a sin. She does not belong to me. I do not want to do it. Forget it, woman!"

## Aim for the better way

Joseph was practical, too. When he saw that this woman was going to do whatever she could to trap him, he broke and ran. The Bible warns us to "flee the evil desires of youth" in 2 Timothy 2:22, and then points to the better way: "Pursue righteousness, faith, love and peace."

If you know someone, an old friend or acquaintance, who is temptation to you, stay away from that person for good! It is not enough to say, "Well, I will tell my husband about it." Or, "I'll pray about it. But you know, what can you do?"

We once gave counsel to a woman, an ordinary, capable person, active in an evangelical church. She had started teaching school part-time. One of the male teachers began making advances toward her. She was shocked! She told her husband and they prayed about it. Her husband told her that when he was tempted, he just pulled out a picture of her and their children and said, "I am married. I love my wife. Forget it."

Then this man made another pass at her. She told him, "Look, I have told my husband. This will bring trouble to you." When he came the third time, however, she gave in, committing immorality not only once, but a second time also. She told me, "I don't feel a heavy guilt about it. I know it's wrong, but I just don't feel that badly about it. I am worried."

It was not enough to tell her husband. She should have quit her job, in my opinion, and fled like Joseph. If you stay where you know that type of temptation exists, where you have felt obvious weakness in your soul, you are inviting trouble. Joseph broke away and ran.

### There is hope

Scripture tells us (Philippians 4:8), "Whatever is true, whatever is noble, whatever is right, whatever is pure, whatever is lovely, whatever is admirable—if anything is excellent or praiseworthy—think about such things." It all begins with a thought. If we can keep our thought life clean, then it is much harder for Satan or temptation to get through. "Whatever is pure, think about such things."

Today, it is so easy to pick up a dirty magazine or book. It is very easy to read corrupt literature. Suggestive, provocative material fills many women's magazines lining grocery store checkout lanes. Television shows flaunt immoral behavior, presenting it as attractive, normal, natural, and good. Corruption defines even news magazines. Therefore, all of us who love the Lord need the mind of Christ to be at work in us.

1 Corinthians 2:16 says, "We have the mind of Christ." The mind of Christ is a pure mind. If we stay away from the corrupting influences, there is no need to go around in panicky fear that we will stumble or fall into temptation. Not only do we have the mind of Christ, but we have the power of Christ. When the mind and power of Christ are at work within us, we have victory over temptation. It is positively and constantly possible. "I can do everything through him who gives me strength" (Philippians 4:13).

However, if we allow our minds to be saturated with impure thoughts, if we fill our minds with trash, we not only begin to daydream but we weaken our will. Slowly, before we know it, we weaken in this tremendous area. It is not easy to speak at this point; but I feel a real burden for the people all around us who are falling into sin and getting divorced. It is hitting close to home.

Therefore, the steps Joseph took are the steps that we must take: First, in our *spirit*—we stand crucified in the presence of the Lord. Next, in our *intellect*—once and for all we settle it: no one belongs to me but my own wife or husband. Finally, in our *will*—with resolve we break and run. Then we have victory!

# Chapter 7

# *The Testing*

*One Bible teacher has pointed out* that every character of the Bible at sometime in life had to be tested by God, first in the most obvious area—the body or the physical, then in the soul, and then in the spirit. When the test in each of these areas had been met successfully, the person was really ready to be God's powerful instrument.

Joseph was tested in the body, physically, and he came through with flying colors. He absolutely overcame with the power of God's presence within him. When his master's wife threw herself at him and made it so inviting for him to commit immorality, Joseph overcame, simply because God was with him and all the power of God was at work in his life.

Next, we see Joseph being tested in his faith and in his intellect. That is, Joseph was being tested in his soul. Intellectually, emotionally, and in his will, he had to be tested. He was going to be used of God to bring an enormous "river of blessing" on his people, upon Egypt and upon the whole world. God had a worldwide view in mind when He chose Joseph; but, before He could use him, He had to test him. He had to test and solidify his faith.

All of us, and most certainly those of us who were fortunate and blessed to be saved when we were boys and girls, have to experience a God-sent testing. None of us likes it. I do not think any normal human being enjoys going through trials and testing. In fact, the Bible says, in Hebrews 12:11, "No discipline seems pleasant at the time, but painful. *Later on,* however, it produces a harvest of righteousness and peace for those who have been trained by it" (italics added). There are just no shortcuts. The Lord has to test and prove us. Years later, when reflecting on our lives, we can tell glowing stories of God's mighty acts on our behalf. But, as we are going through those testings, we find them hard to bear. Even Jesus did. "Although he was a son, he learned obedience from what he suffered" (Hebrews 5:8).

In the Psalms we find a reference to Joseph. Psalm 105:12–22 (NLT) reads:

> He said this when they were few in number,
>     a tiny group of strangers in Canaan.
> They wandered back and forth between nations,
>     from one kingdom to another.
> Yet he did not let anyone oppress them.
>     He warned kings on their behalf:
> "Do not touch these people I have chosen,
>     and do not hurt my prophets."
> He called for a famine on the land of Canaan,
>     cutting off its food supply.
> Then he sent someone to Egypt ahead of them—
>     Joseph, who was sold as a slave.
> There in prison, they bruised his feet with fetters
>     and placed his neck in an iron collar.

Until the time came to fulfill his word,
    the LORD tested Joseph's character.
Then Pharaoh sent for him and set him free;
    the ruler of the nation opened his prison door.
Joseph was put in charge of all the king's household;
    he became ruler over all the king's possessions.
He could instruct the king's aides as he pleased
    and teach the king's advisers.

## The favorite becomes a prisoner again

Joseph, by insulting his master's wife in refusing her advances, made a bitter enemy. She was out to get revenge, and he landed in prison.

Genesis 39:19–23 reads:

> When his master heard the story his wife told him, saying, "This is how your slave treated me," he burned with anger. Joseph's master took him and put him in prison, the place where the king's prisoners were confined.
>
> But while Joseph was there in the prison, the LORD was with him; he showed him kindness and granted him favor in the eyes of the warden. So the warden put Joseph in charge of all those held in the prison, and he was made responsible for all that was done there. The warden paid no attention to anything under Joseph's care, because the LORD was with Joseph and gave him success in whatever he did.

Isn't that fantastic? Even in prison, the Lord prospers Joseph.

God gives him astonishing revelations or unusual responsibilities and then allows him to go through tremendous testing. First, he has early dreams of glory and great power; but then he is sold as a slave. What a contrast! Second, he becomes the manager of the house-

hold of the key assistant to Pharaoh, but then he is falsely accused. Thirdly, he overcomes temptation in the
power of God, and where does he end up? In a filthy
prison. Fourth, we read later, he interprets the dreams of
a fellow prisoner, a key servant of Pharaoh; but, when
that man leaves prison, he forgets his promise to help
release Joseph.

"Couldn't you choose someone else for a change?"

It must have been extremely difficult for this very
young man to understand what God was trying to do
with his life. In the movie, *Fiddler on the Roof*, the main
character, when talking about the Jews being so mis-
treated, looks up to heaven and says, "Lord, I know we
are the chosen people." Then, considering all their troubles and persecutions, with a pleading look in his eyes
he cries, "Couldn't you choose someone else for a
change?"

Sometimes the people of God go through troubles
and problems. "If I am one of the chosen ones, what
would it be like to be one of the unchosen ones?" we are
tempted to say. "Why do I have to go through all this?"
Of course, while health is with us and when things are
going well, that temptation does not come. But when we
go bankrupt, or death strikes or a serious illness affects
us or our loved ones, so many of us immediately lose all
joy. We forget the promises and immediately begin looking toward heaven, asking, "Well, Lord, where are all
those promises?"

We must not forget God's attributes. God is a God
who is in control of the universe. God governs the
world. It may not seem so at times, but He does! And
sometimes, when wars break out and persecution pre-

vails, we may wonder. But be assured, He is in control. No opposition can stand in the way of God's plans; He is supreme and no one can stop Him.

The envy, the hatred, the exile, and the slavery only helped to further the purposes of God in Joseph's life. Joseph's brothers thought, *Aha! Here comes the dreamer. Let's get rid of him and see what will happen to his dreams.*

## Strange road to a throne

Going into slavery took Joseph one step closer to the throne of Egypt. It was a strange route to eminence, but it was God's way for Joseph. God had a plan for him; God had a "top of the world" experience for him.

For every one of us, God has a plan. Dr. Bill Bright of Campus Crusade for Christ put it well in *Four Spiritual Laws*, "God loves you and He has a wonderful plan for your life." For each one of us—man, woman, and child—God has an experience, a job to be done, a ministry that—as far as I am concerned and as far as you are concerned—if you are sensitively walking with the Lord, will be the very best for you. Jeremiah 29:11 says, "'I know the plans I have for you,'" declares the LORD, "'plans to prosper you and not to harm you, plans to give you hope and a future.'" God has something special for each one of us. It is not just wishful thinking; it is the truth.

In Genesis, chapter 15, the Lord had told Abraham that his descendants would be slaves in a foreign country and after 400 years He would bring them out as a wealthy people. So through Joseph, God was accomplishing the details of His covenant made with Abraham many decades before. He was beginning to accomplish His purpose by allowing this teenager to be sold as a slave and transported to Egypt.

### A place for everyone

We know a couple in a little town called Etna in northern California. Only 550 people live in Etna. But, from Etna, the Lord has enabled this couple to reach out to hundreds of people all over the western United States. We have heard testimonies of teens who had been on drugs whom God has delivered through their ministry. One man and his wife travel fifty miles every Sunday just to be ministered to by this couple at the Etna church. To me, their lives have always been a tremendous example of how God can use lives totally given to Him. In a little town of 550, they are in the place of God's appointment and it is amazing what God is doing through them. Something is happening in Etna that is powerful, for the glory of God.

For each of us, the Lord has a special place. When we find that place, the Lord begins to work right through us. We find these words in James 4:6–10:

> He gives us more grace. That is why Scripture says:
>
> "God opposes the proud
>     but gives grace to the humble."
>
> Submit yourselves, then, to God. Resist the devil, and he will flee from you. Come near to God and he will come near to you. Wash your hands, you sinners, and purify your hearts, you double-minded. Grieve, mourn and wail. Change your laughter to mourning and your joy to gloom. Humble yourselves before the Lord, and he will lift you up.

Joseph had big dreams that the Lord gave him— not carnal dreams, but God-given dreams; yet God sent him into slavery. It must have been very hard for him, intellectually and spiritually, to accept this turn of events, to be accused by a wanton, sex-hungry woman and sentenced to jail. But the Lord was with Joseph, who humbled himself before Him, and in due time the Lord exalted him.

The Lord may have given you a vision some time ago, yet the vision never seems to be accomplished. That is what Joseph may have thought, especially during the long months of imprisonment. Time passed and nothing happened. The temptation would be to say, "Lord, what is going on? My brothers hate me. They sold me as a slave. Did I just imagine those promises?"

However, God who governs the world, God who is supreme, who is "the One enthroned in heaven" and laughs (Psalm 2:4), of whom it is written, "Your wrath against men brings you praise" (Psalm 76:10). In accomplishing His will, God can use even our enemies and the circumstances that seem to oppose the fulfillment of His will for our lives.

God sits on His throne, gazing down at His enemies, and He laughs as they frantically scramble around. What a picture! The Lord is not shaken and confused by the enemies of His cause. The Lord is not shaken when we have to go through trials, turbulence and opposition caused by His enemies. He laughs at His enemies. Psalm 76:10 (NKJV) says, "Surely the wrath of man shall praise You." He can take the work of His enemies and turn it around, using it for His glory. That's exciting!

## Is all this necessary?

But what confusion for Joseph! Can you imagine what he was thinking as a slave and later in jail? *Well, Lord, where are all those dreams? What happened? Here I sit*

*in this jail. You told me everybody would bow to me. You told
me that even the stars and the sun and the moon would bow
to me. What am I doing in this jail?* It must have been hard
for him, as it is hard for us when things don't go the way
we think they should.

Early in the history of our evangelistic team we
planned a time of ministry in Spain. It seemed so dis-
couraging. The money was not coming in. I had to go to
Spain without the team members I needed to help with
rallies and meetings. We were not able to buy some of
the equipment and supplies necessary, or pay some of
the expenses we felt we should pay for in Spain.

However, when we arrived, we realized that the
Lord had allowed all this to take place. He gave us a victory for His glory in Spain, despite things not going the
way we thought they should.

Once there, I realized that if I had taken a song
leader, it would have been a waste of money, because
they did not allow us to have singing in the theater. In
many other ways God showed us that He was working
and in control. He gave a great victory!

To our surprise, members of the Spanish Parliament
came to the crusade. People with important government
positions came and listened. They were wide-open to the
gospel. In other words, I went to Spain with a heavy
heart, all alone and very discouraged. But the Lord knew
what He was doing. He was in control. The same can be
true for you.

God's purpose for Joseph's testing in prison was to
make him a man. He had been his father's favorite son,
treated in a special way. Joseph may have been a little
undisciplined, even "spoiled." Although the capacity
was there, the Lord had to allow him to go to prison so

that he would come out of prison as a mature man instead of a boy.

## Wanted: men of steel

Today, we need strong men in the body of Christ. Scripture says, "Be men of courage" (1 Corinthians 16:13). We need men in the churches, in the body of Christ, who are *real men*. All of us need to be made into strong men and women through troubles, tribulations and experiences of delay. And God, who is faithful, will allow us to go through experiences that cause us to emerge as adult men, instead of overgrown boys.

By nature I am an activist. I like to get things done quickly, done right and done my own way. It is very hard for me when people stand in the way, no matter who they are. If someone obstructs my way, my tendency is to bluster and frighten so people will say, "Get out of Luis' way so he can do his thing." It is very hard for me to realize that God's timing is better than my timing, and that God's will is better than my will. The Lord is perfectly capable of achieving His purpose without my human efforts.

Many of us in this era react that way. Joseph may have had these tendencies too. But the Lord knew that famine was coming; therefore, He had to make Joseph a man of steel. He knows what we do not know.

In Psalm 105:18–19 we read: "They bruised his feet with shackles, his neck was put in irons, till what he foretold came to pass, till the word of the LORD proved him true." An old English translation says it this way: "The iron was burnt into his soul." God was molding Joseph, forging him into a man of steel. When he was in jail, the iron was burnt into his soul. Joseph had to become a strong and durable man before God could really use him.

## Let's get moving

Delays are the most frustrating horrors for activists. We just cannot sit still when delays block our progress. We become frustrated. And yet, "we know that in all things God works for the good of those who love him, who have been called according to his purpose" (Romans 8:28). We quote that far too flippantly, don't we? But it is still one of the most potent truths in the whole Bible. All things work together for good to people who trust God and love Him.

The wonderful thing about Joseph was that he did not pull any strings. He did not try to use manipulation. Instead, he just did the right thing, where he was, at the right time. That is so important. His father Jacob tried to manipulate events, but he ended up with a wasted life to look back on. Many others have tried to carnally manipulate matters, and the Lord has had to put them aside until they stop trying to force God's hand through people and events, pulling strings and generally doing things in their own way.

Joseph did not do that. He simply did the right thing where he was. Proverbs 3:5–6 gives a beautiful truth: "Trust in the LORD with all your heart and lean not on your own understanding; in all your ways acknowledge him, and he will make your paths straight." Joseph stayed in jail, did what he had to do, and once again rose to the top. The jailer really had nothing to do with the whole process because God was at work, accomplishing His purposes through the life of Joseph.

## Faithful in the little things

A young man came to two mature Christian men for counsel. He wanted to marry and go to Bible school, but was in debt for $6,000. The answer might seem to be, "Trust in God and go to Bible college." But the very biblical and wise advice given him was, "Do not even consider marriage nor going to college until you pay your debts. Do the right thing first, and stop dreaming about super-spiritual things."

Many of us dream about great spiritual accomplishments, but we do not want to take care of the obvious little everyday details now. I believe that is why so many people are never used of God. Jesus Christ said, "Whoever can be trusted with very little can also be trusted with much" (Luke 16:10). One of the marks of the person who is going to be a leader is that he is faithful in the little things. A person who is willing to pay his bills, keep his house in order and do the right thing now will be honored by God later.

## It's all his (their) fault

Another exciting quality about Joseph was his lack of bitterness toward his brothers and others who treated him unjustly. In Genesis 40:15 he says, "I was forcibly carried off from the land of the Hebrews, and even here I have done nothing to deserve being put in a dungeon."

Did you notice he said, "I was forcibly carried off from the land of the Hebrews"? He does not say, "My treacherous, cowardly brothers sold me and put me in a pit. They *sold* me for twenty shekels!" No, he says simply, "I was stolen." No bitterness whatsoever. Why? Because he saw the hand of God on his life and trusted Him.

Most of us, and I include myself, when we encounter difficulties or obstacles in our path, try to find someone to blame. "If people would get out of my way, I could evangelize 250 million people and then buy a cottage by a lake and retire. But I cannot finish the job God has given me to do because others drag their feet. They do not allow me enough money and they are always standing right in my way."

The Lord is trying to teach me something in this area. I know the truth, yet I must apply it to myself. It is one thing to "know" a principle intellectually; it is another thing, when you are going through a problem, to allow God to have His way.

The late Ray Stedman, for years a well-known pastor from California, once said, "Woe to the man who has to learn principles at the time of crisis." Webster defines "principle" as "fundamental truth or doctrine; settled rule or law of action or conduct." It is good to learn solid, Bible-based principles now, because the crisis will come. The testings will come. They always come. But if you know and apply now the principles of God's Word, when testing comes, you'll have the stability in Christ to stand firm, to go through it, to learn the lesson, and to come out on the other side a fruitful, Spirit-filled person for the glory of the Lord.

### This yoke is not easy

God imposed a heavy yoke on Joseph, but the yoke was the very thing that made him fruitful. When I was seventeen or eighteen, a few years after my father died, I was quite rebellious. "Why were things so hard for us?" I questioned. Many times I complained—to the Lord mostly; but one day I complained to a preacher I knew.

He had a passage for me from Lamentations. It seemed irritating to me at the time, but I have never forgotten it. "It is good for a man to bear the yoke while he is young" (Lamentations 3:27). Somehow, that verse stayed with me. If you bear the yoke from your youth, it is because the Lord has something very special to do through you and you will be prepared.

The Lord says, "Come to me, all you who are weary and burdened, and I will give you rest. Take my yoke upon you and learn from me, for I am gentle and humble in heart, and you will find rest for your souls. For my yoke is easy and my burden is light" (Matthew 11:28–30).

It may seem to those going through troubles that this yoke is not easy. It is heavy! Unfortunately, many times preachers classify the Christian life, insisting, "The Christian life is *hard.* It is very *hard* to follow the Lord. Don't you believe it's easy to be a disciple of Jesus Christ; it is *hard!*"

I want to tell you it is much harder *not* to belong to Christ. The reason the yoke of Christ is an easy yoke is because He shares the yoke with us.

When two oxen are hooked to the plow, the yoke ties them together. Jesus Christ told us, "I am yoked with you. If you take my yoke, my yoke is easy and light." The ones who have a rough time are the unyoked ones. Who helps them carry their burdens? We who are yoked have an easier time because the Lord Jesus pulls together with us.

St. Paul puts it in that beautiful verse, "I have been crucified with Christ and I no longer live, but Christ lives in me. The life I live in the body, I live by faith in the Son of God, who loves me and gave himself for me" (Galatians 2:20).

Joseph had not heard Galatians 2:20, but he knew the experience of being yoked with the Lord. The Lord was with him constantly, encouraging him. Even when Joseph was in jail, the Lord was right there. Joseph went through trouble, tribulation, and anguish, and he came out on top of the world. The Lord suddenly took him out of jail and in a few days he was next to Pharaoh himself. The nation's hero. Why? Because he was yoked to the living God.

No matter what your trouble is, whatever the problems you face, the great secret of victory is simply to "Humble yourselves, therefore, under God's mighty hand, that he may lift you up in due time" (1 Peter 5:6).

Chapter 8

# *Forgive and Forget*

**On the way up again**

While Joseph was still in jail, he interpreted the dreams of Pharaoh's butler and baker. In those days the butler was not just a man who served wine and opened doors; he was one of the Pharaoh's closest assistants. A short while later, as Joseph predicted from the dreams, the baker was hanged and the butler was released.

Then one night, Pharaoh had a dream—all about seven fat cows and seven lean cows. Finally, the butler remembered Joseph's ability to interpret dreams. Pharaoh summoned Joseph, who interpreted the dream as seven productive years and seven years of famine in Egypt. Joseph even suggested what Pharaoh should do to save his people from starvation.

Genesis 41:37–46 (NLT) reads:

Joseph's suggestions were well received by Pharaoh and his advisers. As they discussed who should be appointed for the job, Pharaoh said, "Who could do it better than Joseph? For he is a man who is obviously filled with the spirit of God." Turning to Joseph, Pharaoh said, "Since God has revealed the meaning of the dreams to you, you are the wisest man in the land! I hereby appoint you to direct this project. You will manage my household and organize all my people. Only I will have a rank higher than yours."

And Pharaoh said to Joseph, "I hereby put you in charge of the entire land of Egypt." Then Pharaoh placed his own signet ring on Joseph's finger as a symbol of his authority. He dressed him in beautiful clothing and placed the royal gold chain around his neck. Pharaoh also gave Joseph the chariot of his second-in-command, and wherever he went the command was shouted, "Kneel down!" So Joseph was put in charge of all Egypt. And Pharaoh said to Joseph, "I am the king, but no one will move a hand or a foot in the entire land of Egypt without your approval. "

Pharoah renamed him Zaphenath-paneah and gave him a wife—a young woman named Asenath, the daughter of Potiphera, priest of Heliopolis. So Joseph took charge of the entire land of Egypt. He was thirty years old when he entered the service of Pharaoh, the king of Egypt.

What a position for a young man of thirty. For Joseph to become second in command of the world's greatest empire at thirty, he first had to walk with God in purity and submission from age seventeen. It brings home the fact that if you want to be God's man at thirty, you had better be God's man at seventeen.

The story continues in Genesis 41:46–52, which says:

Joseph went out from Pharoah's presence and trav-
eled throughout Egypt. During the seven years of abundance the land produced plentifully. Joseph collected all
the food produced in those seven years of abundance in
Egypt and stored it in the cities. In each city he put the
food grown in the fields surrounding it. Joseph stored up
huge quantities of grain, like the sand of the sea; it was
so much that he stopped keeping records because it was
beyond measure.

Before the years of famine came, two sons were
born to Joseph by Asenath daughter of Potiphera, priest
of On. Joseph named his firstborn Manasseh and said, "It
is because God has made me forget all my trouble and all
my father's household." The second son he named
Ephraim and said, "It is because God has made me fruitful in the land of my suffering."

Those two things, "forget" and "fruitful," go in
order. If you want to be fruitful, you must forget. And,
when you forget, then God can make you fruitful.

### Here come those brothers
In Genesis 42:1–6 we read:

When Jacob learned that there was grain in Egypt,
he said to his sons, "Why do you just keep looking at
each other?" He continued, "I have heard that there is
grain in Egypt. Go down there and buy some for us, so
that we may live and not die."

Then ten of Joseph's brothers went down to buy
grain from Egypt. But Jacob did not send Benjamin with
the others, because he was afraid that harm might come
to him. So Israel's sons were among those who went to
buy grain, for the famine was in the land of Canaan also.

Now Joseph was the governor of the land, the one
who sold grain to all its people. So when Joseph's brothers arrived, they bowed down to him with their faces to
the ground.

What a scene! At last Joseph's dreams are beginning to come true.

Ah, the irony of God. Those ten fellows never dreamed they were eating dirt in front of their little brother, Joseph. Here they were, bowing before him, with their faces to the ground.

Genesis 42:7–24 reads:

> As soon as Joseph saw his brothers, he recognized them, but he pretended to be a stranger and spoke harshly to them. "Where do you come from?" he asked.
>
> "From the land of Canaan," they replied, "to buy food."
>
> Although Joseph recognized his brothers, they did not recognize him. Then he remembered his dreams about them and said to them, "You are spies! You have come to see where our land is unprotected."
>
> "No, my lord," they answered. "Your servants have come to buy food. We are all the sons of one man. Your servants are honest men, not spies."
>
> "No!" he said to them. "You have come to see where our land is unprotected."
>
> But they replied, "Your servants were twelve brothers, the sons of one man, who lives in the land of Canaan. The youngest is now with our father, and one is no more."
>
> Joseph said to them, "It is just as I told you: You are spies! And this is how you will be tested: As surely as Pharaoh lives, you will not leave this place unless your youngest brother comes here. Send one of your number to get your brother; the rest of you will be kept in prison, so that your words may be tested to see if you are telling the truth. If you are not, then as surely as Pharaoh lives, you are spies!" And he put them all in custody for three days.
>
> On the third day, Joseph said to them, "Do this and you will live, for I fear God: If you are honest men, let one of your brothers stay here in prison, while the rest of

you go and take grain back for your starving households. But you must bring your youngest brother to me, so that your words may be verified and that you may not die." This they proceeded to do.

They said to one another, "Surely we are being punished because of our brother. We saw how distressed he was when he pleaded with us for his life, but we would not listen; that's why this distress has come upon us."

Reuben replied, "Didn't I tell you not to sin against the boy? But you wouldn't listen! Now we must give an accounting for his blood." They did not realize that Joseph could understand them, since he was using an interpreter.

He turned away from them and began to weep . . . .

Years later, when Jacob, the father of Joseph, was about to die, he pronounced a prophecy over each of his twelve sons. In Genesis 49:22–26 we read the prophecy for Joseph:

"Joseph is a fruitful vine,
      a fruitful vine near a spring,
      whose branches climb over a wall.
With bitterness archers attacked him;
      they shot at him with hostility.
But his bow remained steady,
      his strong arms stayed limber,
because of the hand of the Mighty One of Jacob,
      because of the Shepherd, the Rock of Israel,
because of your father's God, who helps you,
      because of the Almighty, who blesses you
with blessings of the heavens above,
      blessings of the deep that lies below,
      blessings of the breast and womb.
Your father's blessings are greater
      than the blessings of the ancient mountains,
      than the bounty of the age-old hills.

Let all these rest on the head of Joseph,
   on the brow of the prince among his brothers."

Jesus Christ said, "You did not choose me, but I
choose you and appointed you to go and bear fruit—
fruit that will last" (John 15:16).

## How to produce fruit

God's will for all men and women is that they
should be fruitful in bringing others to Christ. The
dream of every true Christian is to be a fruit-producing
one. There's nothing more sad than a Christian who simply doesn't produce. God does not want fruit produced
in the energy of the flesh. He doesn't want a "show-offy"
producing, but rather the fruit that comes from God
Himself and is a natural result of a life indwelt by the living Christ.

Joseph, along with many other Bible characters and
even some people alive today, went through enormous
suffering. He was dealt with treacherously. He was
accused falsely. He was criminally forgotten. Yet there
isn't a note of bitterness in his whole life. Because Joseph
saw the hand of God on his life and in his problems and
refused to blame anybody for them, he became a useful
man for the Lord.

He had two sons, Manasseh and Ephraim. The
names fit so well. Manasseh means "forget." When his
first son was born, Joseph called him Manasseh because
he said, "God has made me forget all my trouble and all
my father's household," meaning the bad things. Then,
when he had his second boy, he called him Ephraim
because "God has made me fruitful in the land of my
suffering."

It is very simple to be a fruitful Christian, really. God is in you! God is alive! Christ lives in us! Now why are so many people fruitless? Why don't they produce fruit that glorifies God? One reason, I believe, is that they have not learned to forget. They relive the past, rehash old grievances and fret over wrongs done them. But, until you forget the past, forgive what lies behind and concentrate on the "now" in Christ, you can never bring forth fruit.

## Joseph had every right to be bitter

Joseph had many reasons to be a bitter man, and perhaps you have reasons to be a bitter person. One night after a meeting, my wife and I were stopped by a woman we'd known for years. She looked desperate. Her husband of twenty-seven years had left her. This man, she claimed, was one of the world's biggest hypocrites. He was over fifty now, and she was forty-seven. She had tried to take her life in her desperation. How sad, yet it's hard to blame her. This woman seemingly had every reason to be bitter; but if she continues to nurse this bitterness, she'll never again be a fruitful Christian.

Some of you women have unfaithful husbands. A natural response would be to become bitter. Some of you men have had unfaithful wives. Some of you have been cheated in business by someone calling himself a "brother." Some of you young people have been engaged to someone who suddenly said, "We're through! I don't want you anymore." You seem to have reason to be bitter. Joseph certainly did. But he forgave his brothers with an honest, inner forgiveness. Ephesians 4:32 says, "Be kind and compassionate to one another, forgiving each

other, just as in Christ God forgave you." And in
Romans 12:19, "Do not take revenge, my friends, but
leave room for God's wrath, for it is written: 'It is mine
to avenge; I will repay,' says the Lord."

## Revenge

It is very easy, in the flesh, to seek revenge. By
nature I am a choleric personality type. Cholerics are
known for being vengeful people and, by nature, I am
vengeful.

When I was ten years old, my father died. He left us
quite a bit of property and some money. Certain friends,
who were supposed to be helping us, squandered everything we had. Within three years we were living in utter
poverty and indebtedness because these friends, who
obviously were not Christians, had mismanaged it all, to
their own advantage.

When we got older and really understood what
they had done, my sisters and I tried to urge my mother
to take revenge on them, to get a lawyer to take them to
court and let them have it! The older I got, the more bitter I became. I dreamed vividly of wreaking vengeance
on these men.

But the Bible says that wreaking vengeance is the
Lord's business. He is the one who measures out the jus-
tice. It doesn't mean that He lets people get away with it,
you know. It simply means that it's not our business to
take revenge. He wants to handle such judgment for
us—perhaps now, certainly ultimately.

But my mother always quoted verses about not
going to court, and she forgave them. Even to this day!
Consequently, it took us twenty years to finish paying
our debts. I could never understand why she wouldn't

take them to court.

The lesson my mother taught us by her actions has stayed with me to this day; forty-nine years later I'm still talking about it. She simply refused to take action and she forgot what they did. They're rich now and we are not. But who cares? God has given us a freedom of spirit and opportunities to be fruitful . . . to serve Him . . . to live!

Joseph forgave and forgot. First of all, he forgave. Now, some might say, "Luis, you don't understand. I'm a very sensitive person. I cannot simply—as you say—forget it." Perhaps you say, "Luis, you're a goal-oriented person and you can forget things because you're looking at the goals, but I am very sensitive." What you are really saying is, "I am unforgiving," not sensitive. It's very easy to cover up your unforgiving spirit by calling it "sensitivity" because it sounds much nicer.

Personally, Joseph forgave them fully; but as a man in responsibility, he had to deal with the depth of their sins. He had to do it! All of us who have responsibility over others have to learn this principle, and it's not easy to distinguish between the two. If someone has hurt you, you must forgive him. But as a person in a position of responsibility, you may have to help that one to restore his walk with the Lord. And God will help us do it, hard as it is on most of us to take such initiative.

## Dig out those skeletons

Did you notice that when Joseph dealt harshly with his brothers, they immediately remembered their sins as clearly as if it were yesterday, even though fifteen years had gone by? "'Surely we are being punished because of our brother. We saw how distressed he was when he pleaded with us for his life, but we would not listen; that's why this distress has come upon us'" (Genesis 42:21).

Isn't that interesting? A conscience that is not clear has an incredible memory and it haunts you year after year after year. Maybe you have a skeleton in your closet that you haven't wanted to deal with—some little incident, something you did somewhere, even years ago, that's never been made right. Until you settle it, you can never be fruitful for God.

These fellows, Joseph's brothers, not only remembered, but they went at each other's throats again, viciously accusing one another. Immediately Reuben turns to his brothers and points a finger. "Didn't I tell you," he said, "not to sin against the lad? But you would not listen. So now comes a reckoning for his blood."

I can just imagine Joseph looking compassionately at them and listening to them argue among themselves. They were not mature men, they were just—old men. Spiritually, they were babies. When Joseph heard them arguing, he was so shaken that he left the room and cried.

That's a beautiful picture. A person who forgives others weeps, not for the harm done to him, but for the foolish immaturity of the other person. Putting myself in Joseph's place, humanly speaking, I know what I would do. I'd stand up there and say, "You traitors, do you know who I am? I'm Joseph, the brother you wronged. Now I'm on top of the world, and I'm going to let you have what you deserve."

But not Joseph. What a beautiful lesson. Joseph doesn't say anything because he is God's man. He wants to deal with the depths of their consciences. He goes away and weeps in a back room.

The Bible says, "'If your enemy is hungry, feed him; if he is thirsty, give him something to drink'" (Romans 12:20).

Do you remember when the brothers left for the trip home? Joseph had told his men to fill the sacks with more grain and to "replace every man's money in his sack." When they opened their sacks and saw not only more grain than they had bought, but also the money returned, their guilty consciences misinterpreted even these gifts.

Instead of saying, "Praise God, I don't know why he did it, but I'm $20 richer," a person with a guilty conscience says, "Why did he do that? He's trying to buy me off." A guilty conscience always misinterprets even the best gifts.

### "I am Joseph, your brother"

Then finally, in Genesis 44:16–18 we read:

> "What can we say to my lord?" Judah replied. "What can we say? How can we prove our innocence? God has uncovered your servants' guilt. We are now my lord's slaves—we ourselves and the one who was found to have the cup."
>
> But Joseph said, "Far be it for me to do such a thing! Only the man who was found to have the cup will become my slave. The rest of you, go back to your father in peace."
>
> Then Judah went up to him and said: "Please, my lord, let your servant speak a word to my lord. Do not be angry with your servant, though you are equal to Pharaoh himself."

Here is old Judah, completely broken. He becomes a spokesman for his brothers. Finally, they are genuinely broken for their sins. Finally, they realize that the sin of selling Joseph years before, which was the picture of all their sinfulness, has been found out. They are repentant. They are frightened. They realize they have ruined their lives. They break down before Joseph, and it is then that Joseph reveals himself to them.

True repentance is full disclosure. When they were finally broken, Joseph said, "I am Joseph, your brother; don't be afraid. Is my father all right?"

Jesus Christ said, "Blessed are the pure in heart, for they will see God" (Matthew 5:8). The thing that obscures our vision of God is guilt on our conscience. Whenever we have something on our conscience that has not been properly cleared, disclosed and confessed, we lose our vision of God.

Joseph, by being able to forgive his brothers, was able to disclose himself to them, to be open and honest with them. We remember Joseph's sons, Manasseh (forget) and Ephraim (fruitful). When Joseph had forgiven his brothers, he was able to forget. Only after you forget can you produce fruit for God's glory. If you keep remembering incidents and constantly trying to cast blame and explain yourself to others, let me lovingly warn you. If you cannot settle it, bury it. Forget it. Otherwise, you are not only going to be stifled spiritually for the rest of your life, but you'll be unfruitful and unproductive, as well.

And remember, you must also forgive yourself. Many people carry heavy burdens of guilt unnecessarily when God has forgiven them, but they cannot accept His forgiveness. That is not God's will for your life. He doesn't want your life to be stagnant from living in the past. He wants you to be fruitful. So, first of all, forgive in the power of Christ, as God in Christ has forgiven you; and secondly, forget it.

The apostle Paul said in Philippians 3:13–14, "Brothers, I do not consider myself yet to have taken hold of it. But one thing I do: Forgetting what is behind and straining toward what is ahead, I press on toward the goal to win the prize for which God has called me heavenward in Christ Jesus."

Forget it and strain forward to what God has before you.

In Hebrews 12:15 we read, "See to it that no one misses the grace of God and that no bitter root grows up to cause trouble and defile many." If you allow a "root of bitterness" to spring up in your life, then not only do you cause trouble, but many people will be defiled by your attitude and actions.

Now you might say, "Oh, Luis, that's easy for you to say because everything's going fine for you." It isn't so fine sometimes. But that is not the point. It is the Lord speaking to you. He says, "See to it that no 'root of bitterness' springs up." Joseph absolutely forgot and as a result he was a tremendously fruitful blessing to the rest of the people.

All of us experience potentially devastating experiences. A root of bitterness can bring generations of unhappiness, and the issues at stake are not worth the weight given them nor the mental anguish they cause.

I recall an older Christian woman, successful in so many ways, the mother of four grown children, who never engaged in prolonged conversation without referring to childhood sadness, far in the past. Her mother had died and her father had remarried. She never really forgave him for this, and her mind worked double-time recalling incidents of slights and hurts on the part of the now-deceased stepmother. The interesting, though sad, thing now is to see the absolute, certain fulfillment of a biblical warning "that many be defiled." The second generation, four children now forming homes of their own, suffers from this same tendency to be long of memory regarding injustices; and four more homes are not all that God intended them to be. Little plants have such deep roots.

Joseph saw the sovereign, merciful hand of God at work across the pages of history. He said, "You intended to harm me, but God intended it for good." That is why he could forget. Because he could ignore the human circumstances and look to the God behind them. The result—Joseph had peace. He could see and trust the hand of God behind the scenes.

Scripture tells us that God said, "Their sins and lawless acts I will remember no more" (Hebrews 10:17). Someone has said, "The God who knows everything is able to forgive everything and forget it all." That's amazing! And He can help you and me to forget and look forward to the future.

Will you forget the past and become a fruitful person? That is the key to fulfilling God's purpose for you.

The Lord Jesus said, and never forget this, "You did not choose me, but I chose you to go and bear fruit— fruit that will last" (John 15:16).

# Chapter 9

# Joseph, A Picture of Christ

### God is still in control

We have been looking at God at work in the life of
Joseph. We have seen, first of all, the sovereignty of
God—God Almighty putting His hand on this boy
Joseph and giving him a dream, electing him, calling
him, showing Himself to Joseph and saying, "Joe, boy,
I've got something for you. I am going to give you a lit-
tle glimpse of it." He gives him a dream when he is sev-
enteen, and yet another dream later on.

Then we saw the hand of God in the life of Joseph
operating as the government of God. God in control of
every activity—God supreme, overruling and overcom-
ing the opposition of all the enemies who were trying to
stand in the way of Joseph's progress.

We saw God's permissive will, allowing Joseph to
be sold as a slave, allowing Joseph to be tempted by the

woman, allowing Joseph to be taken into jail. We saw God's faithfulness, standing by Joseph, making him go to the top at Potiphar's house and then allowing him to go down again. We saw a God full of promises.

We saw Joseph operating in the Spirit of God by the forgiveness that he extended to his brothers. He absolutely forgave them. There was no bitterness at all in his heart. Not once did he recriminate them. Not once did he act as if he were going to take revenge. Not at all! That was the hand of God upon Joseph.

### Preach to the conscience

Years ago, when I began to study the Bible, preparing myself to preach, I read books by John Nelson Darby. He said, "Whenever you preach, you must preach to the conscience." That is the duty of a preacher. If we are going to help people, we must touch the conscience—not in an accusatory sort of way, but in a way that ministers in the spirit so that the conscience comes alive.

The conscience was certainly alive in Joseph's brothers. They remembered after fifteen years exactly what they had done to Joseph and exactly what Joseph said when they shoved him into the pit. It was their conscience that caused them to start fighting among themselves. Joseph's strange method of dealing with them brings out their consciences.

It almost seems cruel what he did to them, particularly what he did to Benjamin. Why did he do it? Why did he put his special cup in Benjamin's sack and then, when the brothers had left the city, send some guards to stop them by saying, "Halt! Somebody has stolen our master's cup." But it hadn't been stolen, it had been intentionally put in Benjamin's sack. The guards searched diligently and found it. Then the brothers all had to come back and stand in front of Joseph again (Genesis 44:1–13).

### It's the attitude that counts

Why did Joseph pick on Benjamin, his own blood brother whom he loved? Joseph went through all that rigmarole of bringing them back and pretending he didn't know who they were because he had to deal with their consciences. There were two attitudes that he wanted to examine in their lives.

One was their attitude toward their father. They had been cruel to their father. They had proved at Shechem (Genesis 34) that they were violent men. He knew that they must have lied to their father and broken his heart when they had tried to explain his own disappearance. Joseph wanted to know if they were broken and repentant for that.

Second, he wanted to discern their attitude toward Benjamin. Benjamin was Joseph's one and only blood-brother, 100 percent. His father had started treating him as he used to treat Joseph. So Joseph wanted to know if the brothers had changed their attitude toward Benjamin, who was a picture—as it were—of Joseph himself. Therefore, he forced the issue by making it appear that their troubles now were Benjamin's fault. Since they did not know who Joseph was and they did not know that he could understand their language, they would surely betray their true feelings.

What he did to them may seem cruel, but sometimes the conscience needs to be dealt with cruelly. These men were tough men. They did not break down easily. Joseph knew it. Therefore, he had to really let them have it before they finally came groveling, not so much before him, but before God.

Judah, the brother who spoke for the others, comes crawling: "'What can we say to my lord?' Judah replied. 'What can we say? How can we prove our innocence? God has uncovered your servants' guilt. We are now my lord's slaves—we ourselves and the one who was found to have the cup'" (Genesis 44:16). Finally they were broken. Joseph says to himself, "At last. Now I can reveal myself to them."

## Substitution and restitution

Some of you may have a problem with the forgiveness of your sins or the erasure of your guilt. Someone said to me, "You know, it's easier for me to know that God has forgiven me, than to forgive myself." It is easier to know that your wife forgives you for what you did than to forgive yourself. If you find it hard to believe and accept that God and others have forgiven you, so as to have utter peace with Him, there are two words I pass on to you. One is substitution and the other is restitution.

*Substitution* means that you not only believe that something happened on the cross, that God placed your sins on Jesus Christ, but also that you yourself, by faith, take your sins and place them on Jesus Christ. That is what Scripture teaches. That Jesus Christ took upon Himself the sin that you cannot forgive; so that, since God has forgiven you, you can forgive yourself. But in your heart I believe you must go through that simple step where you, by faith, place it on the Lord Jesus because that is what the Father did on the cross.

Another step involves the reason that so many people cannot forgive themselves and be totally truthful.

That is *restitution*. You must go back and settle it totally with the person you have hurt. If it is a girlfriend you wronged years ago and it will not leave your conscience, you must go and settle it. If it is a dirty business deal and you know you did wrong, although perhaps no one else does and the law will never get you, go back and settle it.

What they did to Joseph had happened fifteen years before. Joseph had no revenge in his heart. He couldn't care less anymore. He was on top of the world. Besides, his heart was totally forgiving. But *they* needed to settle that affair. Until you settle it, you cannot have total peace; nor can you be a fruitful Christian. And it may not be a big thing either.

## A box of crayons

While growing up, I attended a British boarding school in Argentina. I did many wrong things, but one of them God used to really get through to me. I stole a box of crayons. I took it from a young fellow, a son of missionaries. The little box didn't cost more than fifty cents, but it proved to be a big thing in my life.

When I started walking closer to the Lord, I would be praying and studying the Bible and every once in a while a little voice would say, "How about that box of crayons you stole?" It was God the Holy Spirit speaking to me. It seemed like such a stupid, minor thing, but it actually was a problem I needed to settle. I said, "Lord, if I could find that fellow, I would give him ten boxes of crayons. I *want* to tell him that I stole those crayons from him!"

One day, when I was twenty-six years old and married, we went to the Bay Area of San Francisco, California, and somebody said, "You have an invitation to speak at a Brethren chapel across the Bay. One of the elders by the name of So-and-so."

"Ohhh," I said. "I can't believe it! Can it be the same John from school days in Argentina?"

"He wants you to have dinner at his house," they said.

So I went, and it was he! I had to make my confession. It was kind of ridiculous, of course. He looked at me and he said, "Forget it, I don't need any crayons!" But I felt so good. Never again would I have to kneel beside my bed to pray and hear that Voice say, "How about those crayons, Luis?" I had settled my conscience problem by simple confession and a willingness to repay. And what peace I began to have.

Joseph may have seemed cruel. But the sin that brings on the guilt is usually cruel too. Certainly, restitution can be very hard and it seems cruel that God would expect us to go back and pay. But think how cruel you were, in many ways, when you did the thing in the first place.

### Do your boughs spill over the wall?
What a fruitful person Joseph became.
Genesis 49:22–26 reads:

"Joseph is a fruitful vine,
　　a fruitful vine near a spring,
　　whose branches climb over a wall.
With bitterness archers attacked him;
　　they shot at him with hostility.
But his bow remained steady,
　　his strong arms stayed limber,
because of the hand of the Mighty One of Jacob,
　　because of the Shepherd, the Rock of Israel.

Because of your father's God, who helps you,
        because of the Almighty, who blesses you
with blessings of the heavens above,
        blessings of the deep that lies below,
        blessings of the breast and womb.
Your father's blessings are greater
        than the blessings of the ancient mountains,
        than the bounty of the age-old hills.
Let all these rest on the head of Joseph,
        on the brow of the prince among his brothers.

Are you a fruitful Christian? Do your boughs spill over the wall? When you meet people, are you a blessing to them? Or are you one of those groveling Christians who is always looking for a blessing, always searching for counsel? When we are going through troubles, we all need counseling, of course; but for some people such dependence becomes a habit. They cling to others who are "branches of God" like spiritual monkeys and never produce themselves. They are never a spiritual blessing to others.

God wants you and me to be fruitful boughs. There are enough desperate people around. Get off the branches! Become a bough yourself! The Lord wants us to be fruitful. Scripture says, "I am the vine; you are the branches. If a man remains in me and I in him, he will bear much fruit; apart from me you can do nothing" (John 15:5).

And again, "You did not choose me, but I chose you and appointed you to go and bear fruit—fruit that will last" (John 15:16).

### God made Joseph fruitful from his youth

When a person decides as a teenager to serve God, he can be fruitful from the very beginning. You do not have to wait, to start in your old age. Some do, the unfortunate ones. The ones who are blessed start young. They are fruitful from their youth, as was Joseph.

Look at the fruit. First, he had dreams that were answered; second, he manifested the Spirit of God. You remember that even the pagan Pharaoh admitted, "What man is there who has the Spirit of God like this man?" Third, he became second in the land. Actually, he was the highest because Pharaoh was a figurehead. Fourth, he saved Egypt and all the earth from hunger and destruction. Fifth, he was fruitful in that he had a happy family. God gave him a wife and two sons. Obviously this is the picture of a very fruitful and happy family. I have no doubt that Joseph brought that pagan wife to faith in the living God.

Sixth, he was fruitful in that he protected his own father and his brothers from starvation. Seventh, he was an instrument of God's purpose. He was a spearhead of God to take Israel into Egypt, to fulfill the promises of God given to Abraham in Genesis 15. Eighth, he sought his father's blessing for his boys and he was a joy to his father. Ninth, out of one tribe, he became two tribes. What a double blessing the Lord gave him and what double fruit! All the other tribes remained with one name, the original name. But God subdivided Joseph and He used Joseph's sons to multiply his influence.

Remember the day when Jacob said, "Israel shall bless himself by the name of your boys"? Jacob had finished his years in Egypt. He is dying and Joseph and his two sons request an audience.

Genesis 48:8–12 reads:

When Israel saw the sons of Joseph, he asked, "Who are these?"

"They are the sons God has given me here," Joseph said to his father.

Then Israel said, "Bring them to me so I may bless them."

Now Israel's eyes were failing because of old age, and he could hardly see. So Joseph brought his sons close to him, and his father kissed them and embraced them.

Israel said to Joseph, "I never expected to see your face again, and now God has allowed me to see your children too."

Then Joseph removed them from Israel's knees and bowed down with his face to the ground.

Joseph, at this point, was the second in command in the whole world. No one else was in the room. Joseph came with his sons when he heard that his father was about to die. He asked for an audience with his father. Even though he was top man in the country before whom everyone bowed and saluted, Joseph himself went humbly to his old father. He closed the door, took his two little sons off Jacob's knees and he "bowed down with his face to the ground."

### Jacob gives his blessing

There was Joseph, the top person in the world. And there was the old man—all bent over, twisted, and blind. But it was his father. He had a tremendous respect for his father. He was a man of God, for all his weaknesses. And the big man of the world, Joseph, went down on his knees and threw himself in front of his father. Why? He is asking his father to bless his sons. It is a great scene. Continuing with Genesis 48:13–16, we read:

Joseph took both of them, Ephraim on his right toward Israel's left hand and Manasseh on his left toward Israel's right hand, and brought them close to him. But Israel reached out his right hand and put it on Ephraim's head, though he was the younger, and crossing his arms, he put his left hand on Manasseh's head, even though Manasseh was the firstborn.

Then he blessed Joseph and said,

"May the God before whom my fathers
    Abraham and Isaac walked,
the God who has been my shepherd
    all my life to this day,
the Angel who has delivered me from all harm
    —may he bless these boys.
May they be called by my name
    and the names of my fathers Abraham and Isaac,
and may they increase greatly upon the earth."

In those days, the blessing of the father, especially of a patriarch, meant a great deal. It was not just that the one to whom he gave the blessing received the inheritance, in the same way a will does today. The blessing encompassed a spiritual dimension, also. When the father or the grandfather gave a blessing with his right hand, it represented a touch of God. It was most important. The idea was that the firstborn was the one who received the special blessing for family leadership.

However, many times in the Bible you find this crossing of hands. "Jacob have I loved, but Esau have I hated." Jacob was the younger and Esau was the older. Now Jacob was going to bless Joseph's sons and Joseph maneuvered them. He thought, "The old man can't see. If he is going to put his right hand on the one to whom it belongs, the oldest son, I had better put him on his right side." But the old man crossed his hands and was going to bless the younger one over the older.

Genesis 48:17–22 reads:

> When Joseph saw his father placing his right hand on Ephraim's head he was displeased; so he took hold of his father's hand to move it from Ephraim's head to Manasseh's head. Joseph said to him, "No, my father, this one is the firstborn; put your right hand on his head."
>
> But his father refused and said, "I know, my son, I know. He too will become a people, and he too will become great. Nevertheless, his younger brother will be greater than he, and his descendants will become a group of nations." He blessed them that day and said,
>
> "In your name will Israel
>    pronounce this blessing:
> 'May God make you like Ephraim
>    and Manasseh.'"
>
> So he put Ephraim ahead of Manasseh.
>
> Then Israel said to Joseph, "I am about to die, but God will be with you and take you back to the land of your fathers. And to you, as one who is over your brothers, I give the ridge of land I took from the Amorites with my sword and my bow."

## Modern-day blessings

I think there is something in the soul of every man that we Westerners are very loath to confess, and it is that we love and want, perhaps secretly, the blessing of an older man. I do, I will be honest with you.

I believe we all would love that, even though we think it may seem to be a sign of weakness. In the Old

Testament, it was a big thing. The biggest question in life was, "Who is going to put his hands on the child, in blessing?"

Some of us who are getting older, I feel, ought to take seriously this business of being "fathers in Christ." Scripture speaks, in 1 John 2 of "dear children, young men, fathers." I would like to be a father—the sooner the better, spiritually speaking.

A ten-year-old boy once came up and talked with me. I put my hand on his head. I did not give him any blessing, but I began to think. It is something solemn when a man who loves God and walks with God puts his hand on your head and says, "I believe God is going to use you." You never forget it.

When I first came to the USA, a man from California, a respectable elder in a local church, took me aside one day. He said, "Luis, I believe that the Lord is going to use you to bring millions of people to Jesus Christ. I expect to live to see it happen." To me that was from the Lord. I have never forgotten it. And it has already taken place in a great measure. That word of blessing from a spiritual leader sealed something deep in my soul.

I do not believe we can casually experiment with this but I believe there is a time when we might practice it in the name of the Lord.

When Charles Spurgeon, the famous nineteenth-century British preacher, was six years old, a preacher came to his grandfather's house. At breakfast one morning, this preacher took the little boy Charles, sat him on his knee and said, "I believe that this little boy will be used of God to preach the gospel to all of England and win thousands upon thousands to Jesus Christ." He was only six, but he never forgot it. He started preaching at sixteen. At twenty, he was preaching to 20,000 people.

After that breakfast, the preacher took that little boy to a grove in the grandfather's garden. He sat him down and for two hours he gave him counsel. That is really something, isn't it? We tend to look at a six-year-old and say, "Go play, boy; get out of my way." But this preacher noticed Spurgeon and gave him counsel, and Spurgeon became one of the greatest Bible preachers of all time.

## Spiritual babies

I think some of us need to stop being spiritual babies and become spiritual fathers. The world needs it badly.

One day we were making a short television movie in one of the secular movie-producing studios. While there, I noticed a poster that really made me laugh. It was announcing a film titled, *Dirty Little Billy*. It included a picture of Billy the Kid dressed up in a ridiculously long coat and hat. Underneath the title on the poster I read, "Billy the Kid was a punk!"

I thought, "Oh, Lord, when I die, I hope when my Board of Directors get together and are joking around, they won't have to say, 'Luis Palau was a punk!'"

Unfortunately, however, many of us, if we were honest, would have to say we are just nothing but spiritual babies. How awful! God wants us to be fathers! To me, it is most touching to see Joseph, flat on his face, putting his two little sons in front of the old grandfather, saying, "Give them a blessing, Father."

We do not take seriously enough these little boys and girls and young people who admire us more than we realize. They come up and kind of say, "Hi . . . ."

Do you know something? Lately, I have become more aware of this. When a little boy runs by and calls out, "Hi, Luis," and runs away, I try to get his name and catch him later, because the Lord prompted the child to greet me, I believe.

All of us have a spiritual authority that we never use or sometimes we only play around with. What a blessing we can be to others, as others have been to us.

My father died when I was ten, so I have always transferred this authority concept to my mother. If my mother approves of something, I don't care what the rest of the world thinks. If she says "Praise the Lord," I don't care who criticizes. She is my mother!

Every one of us has a responsibility to widows and orphans who do not have a father. We have a responsibility to the children of divorced people, to be "fathers in Jesus Christ" to them. And the blessing that an unfaithful husband did not give his own children, we are to supply as God's men and women.

## To be like Christ

The final and crowning glory of Joseph and his fruitfulness was what I will call, "the figure principle": First, forgiveness; second, forgetfulness; third, fruitfulness; and fourth, the figure principle. This was Joseph's greatest glory.

Joseph was a thrilling type, or figure, of our Lord Jesus Christ. Someone has said that if you study Scripture, you will find 400 parallels between the life of Joseph and the life of our Lord Jesus Christ. Joseph resembles the Lord Jesus Christ. Our God is a transforming God, a God who loves to transform people's characters. He loves to get into your life and my life and make us whole persons, persons like Jesus Christ. He wants to make you and me men and women of God.

The crowning glory of Joseph was that with God at work in and through him, he so beautifully mirrored the Lord.

The greatest prayer I have is that my wife, my sons, the team members I work with, and the people who are closest to my heart will, as the years go by, see more and more of the character and the characteristics of Jesus Christ in my life. Every man and woman who belongs to the Lord Jesus should have that inner desire.

St. Paul expressed that desire for others in Galatians 4:19, saying, "My dear children, for whom I am again in the pains of childbirth until Christ is formed in you." That is God's design to form Christ in me and in you.

In 2 Corinthians 3:18, we read, "We, who with unveiled faces all reflect the Lord's glory, are being transformed into his likeness with ever-increasing glory, which comes from the Lord, who is the Spirit." As we take off the mask, as we stop the pretense and begin to walk openly with God, as we look with unveiled face at the Lord, we are being transformed from one degree of glory to another.

## But how?

In 1 Thessalonians 5:24 we read, "The one who calls you is faithful and he will do it." The Lord will do it! He called you, and He will do it! You can trust Him to do it! With some of us, it is going to take longer than with others because we are stubborn. Yet, the Lord will do it if we will cooperate with Him and allow Him to work in us, and the sooner the better.

First of all, in comparing the life of Joseph with that of Jesus Christ, we notice that Joseph was loved by his father and honored over the others. Likewise, Jesus was honored by His Father.

Second, Joseph was hated by his brothers and sold treacherously for twenty shekels; yet he was honored by some of the Gentiles. John 1:11–12 says, referring to Jesus, "He came to that which was his own, but his own did not receive him. Yet to all who received him, to those who believed in his name, he gave the right to become children of God."

Third, Joseph was accused falsely, but he made no response and was sent to prison. Likewise, the Lord Jesus, who was accused falsely, did not respond and was subsequently sent to the cross.

Fourth, Joseph was put in prison with two law-breakers. One of them was condemned; but the other was saved.

Fifth, Joseph was apparently buried and forgotten. The Lord Jesus was also buried and His enemies thought they were rid of Him. But on the third day He rose again.

Sixth, Joseph was raised to the highest honor. When Pharaoh paraded him down the streets, the leaders went ahead and said, "Bow the knee, bow the knee." Every Egyptian had to bow before Joseph, a Hebrew. So with Jesus; Scripture says, "At the name of Jesus every knee should bow" (Philippians 2:10).

Last of all, Joseph saved millions from starvation and he was able to bring his own people into a land of plenty and set them aside in a special place. In the same way, the Lord Jesus has saved millions of us from eternal condemnation and has a special place for the Jewish people.

Those are just some points—and they are limited parallels—to remind us that Joseph was a beautiful figure and picture of the Lord Jesus Christ. What a privilege to even slightly resemble Him. The secret lies in the unveiled face. "We, who with unveiled faces all reflect the Lord's glory, are being transformed into his likeness with ever-increasing glory" (2 Corinthians 3:18).

May our eyes be fixed upon the Lord Jesus!

> Once it was the blessing,
>     Now it is the Lord.
> Once it was the feeling,
>     Now it is His word.
> Once His gift I wanted,
>     Now the Giver own.
> Once I sought for healing,
>     Now Himself alone.
> Once 'twas painful trying,
>     Now 'tis perfect trust.
> Once a half salvation,
>     Now the uttermost.
> Once 'twas ceaseless holding,
>     Now He holds me fast.
> Once 'twas constant drifting,
>     Now my anchor's cast.
> Once it was my workings,
>     His it hence shall be.
> Once I tried to use Him,
>     Now He uses me.
> Once the power I wanted,
>     Now the Mighty One.
> Once for myself I labored,
>     Now for Him alone.
> All in all forever,
>     Jesus will I sing.
> Everything in Jesus,
>     And Jesus everything.
> —A. B. Simpson

# Wrap up

*There you have it!* The J-J File. Jacob and Joseph. The Schemer and the Dreamer. The one who connived and maneuvered and the one who trusted. God loved both of them very much, and used them for His glory. Eventually, even Jacob was useful when he was wrestled into submission.

Most of us will not have 130 years in which to scheme. In fact, in view of world conditions, it is possible that we have only a short time to serve the Lord before He returns.

God wants to use us. He has our lives planned out perfectly—to serve Him—win souls—be fruitful—experience an abundant life—be transformed into the image of Jesus Christ—for His glory.

He has it planned, but the plan could take years to fulfill if we insist on being wrestled into submission, rather than humbling ourselves willingly under the mighty hand of God. Wrestling is hard work. It saps the energy. Joseph did not argue; he didn't try to run things his way. Instead, he channeled his energy into trust, and look at what God did through him!

God can use you like that. He wants to! The world around us is crying for trusting, fruitful Josephs; but, unfortunately, the church is full of stubborn, balking Jacobs.

What will you be? A Jacob or a Joseph?

Won't you make your decision now?

# Recommended Reading

To further enrich your Christian life, look for the following books in your local Christian bookstore. If the store doesn't have one of these books in stock, ask the sales clerk to order it for you.

*Authentic Christianity* by Ray C. Stedman (Discovery House Publishers)

*Body Life* by Ray C. Stedman (Discovery House Publishers)

*Calling America and the Nations to Christ* by Luis Palau (Thomas Nelson Publishers)

*God Is Relevant* by Luis Palau and David Sanford (Doubleday)

*God's Loving Word: Exploring the Gospel of John* by Ray C. Stedman (Discovery House Publishers)

*Healthy Habits for Spiritual Growth* by Luis Palau (Discovery House Publishers)

*A Life of Integrity* by Howard Hendricks, general editor (Multnomah Books)

*Luis Palau* by W. Terry Whalin (Bethany House Publishers)

*A Man After God's Heart* by Luis Palau (Discovery House Publishers)

*More Than Conquerors* by John Woodbridge, general editor (Moody Press)

*The Only Hope for America* by Luis Palau with Mike Umlandt (Crossway Books)

*The Peter Promise* by Luis Palau with Ellen Bascuti (Discovery House Publishers)

*Say Yes! How to Renew Your Spiritual Passion* by Luis Palau (Discovery House Publishers)

*Seven Promises of a Promise Keeper* by Luis Palau, et al. (Focus on the Family Publishing)

*Sharing Christ When You Feel You Can't* by Daniel Owens (Crossway Books)

*Where Was God When . . . ?* by Luis Palau with Steve Halliday (Doubleday)

*Your New Life with Christ* by Luis Palau (Crossway Books)

# About the Author

Who is Luis Palau? Perhaps you've followed his ministry with interest for years. Or perhaps this book is your first introduction to the man.

Luis Palau is now becoming well known in his adopted homeland, America. His popularity in Latin America, the United Kingdom, and other parts of the world is rather remarkable.

During one crusade, more than 518,000 people in London turned out to hear Luis Palau in person. And, a few years ago, a crowd of 700,000 people gathered to hear Luis on Thanksgiving Sunday in Guatemala.

In many ways, Luis Palau stands out in this generation as a truly international Christian spokesman and leader. He's a third-generation transplanted European who grew up in the province of Buenos Aires, Argentina, and then chose to become an American citizen after completing the graduate course at Multnomah Biblical Seminary in Portland, Oregon.

Equally fluent in English and Spanish, Luis Palau's solidly biblical, practical messages hit home in the minds and hearts of listeners around the world.

"Luis is probably more in demand among evangelicals to preach and speak than almost any other person in the world," says Billy Graham. "Wherever there is an evangelical conference they try to get Luis Palau, because he is a powerful preacher. But more than that, he is an evangelist to whom God has given a multiplicity of gifts."

Luis Palau has proclaimed the Good News of Jesus Christ to hundreds of millions of people via radio and television in 103 countries, and face-to-face to more than 13 million people on 6 continents.

The impact? Many hundreds of thousands of people have trusted Jesus Christ and become established as disciples in local churches. Cities and nations have heard a clear-cut proclamation of the gospel. Luis Palau's burden is to see the same thing happen in America, in this generation.

Luis and his wife, Pat, also a popular conference speaker and author, have served as missionary-evangelists in Costa Rica, Colombia, and Mexico. The Palaus have four grown sons and now make their home in Portland, Oregon, near the international headquarters of the Luis Palau Evangelistic Association.

# *Correspondence*

If this book has motivated you to earnestly follow God, surrendering to Him, or if you have been helped in any other way through the varied ministries of the Luis Palau Evangelistic Association, please let me know. I'd love to hear from you! My address is:

Luis Palau
P.O. Box 1173
Portland, OR 97207, U.S.A.
lpea@palau.org
http://www.gospelcom.net/lpea

# *Note to the Reader*

The publisher invites you to share your response to the message of this book by writing to Discovery House Publishers, P.O. Box 3566, Grand Rapids, MI 49501, USA. For information about other Discovery House books, music, or videos, contact us at the same address or call 1-800-653-8333. Find us on the Internet at http://www.dhp.org/ or send an e-mail to books@dhp.org.